1972

FATALISM IN THE WORKS
OF THOMAS HARDY

FATALISM
IN THE WORKS OF
THOMAS HARDY

ALBERT PETTIGREW ELLIOTT

NEW YORK / RUSSELL & RUSSELL

1966

CONTENTS

FOREWORD

So much has been written about Hardy's philosophy since the end of the last century that one is justified in hesitating to expound its tenets or to derive it from critics and thinkers of the past. This present study attempts to do neither of these things. Nor does it propose to repeat or refute the findings of Brennecke, Hedgecock, Duffin, Garwood, Swann, or any of the others who have attempted to define Hardy's relation to philosophy. It is interested only in a general way with the man as a philosopher. Its chief concern is with Hardy the artist, and with an analysis of his art in its relation to Fate as an artistic motif. A thorough attempt to accumulate data for such a study of his work has never before been made.

The basis of this thesis is a very careful study of Hardy's verse and prose, assisted by a careful reading of accessible books written about him. Its chief value, if value it has, consists in the collection, arrangement, and interpretation of concrete instances of various uses of Fate gathered from his published works. To this end, the main body of my work is an elaborate collection of such excerpts, rather than the usual generalizations of the subject. It is to be hoped that such an amassing of data will eventually result in reaching a more accurate understanding of Hardy's philosophy and the nature of its growth.

My chief concern has been to show that Hardy's conception of Fate as an artistic motif divides naturally into a series of distinct, yet related themes, which run through his books from the beginning of his literary career.

My interest in Hardy began several years ago when I was a student under the late Professors John Leslie Hall of the College of William and Mary, and Edwin Greenlaw of Johns Hopkins University. To both of these men I owe a great deal. To Professor Cornelius Weygandt of the University of Pennsylvania, I am indebted for stimulation and guidance in this study. It has been written under his kind supervision and direction. My former classmate, Mr. Robert Warnock, of Yale University, has given valuable aid in organizing and handling much difficult material. His advice has been of much value. To Mr. Charles R. Flack, Librarian of Southwestern Louisiana Institute, I am grateful for aid in securing out-of-the-way books, for calling my attention to matters that might otherwise have escaped me, and for his other acts of kindness.

Lafayette, Louisiana
March 18, 1932   A. P. E.

ACKNOWLEDGEMENTS TO PUBLISHERS

Publishers of Thomas Hardy's novels and poems and of books dealing with his works have been generous in allowing me to use material from their various editions. Acknowledgement is made to the following publishing houses: To Macmillian Co. for the right to quote from *Wessex Poems, Time's Laughingstocks, Satires of Circumstance, Poems of the Past and Present, Moments of Vision, Late Lyrics and Earlier, Human Shows, Far Phantasies* and *Winter Words.* All of these except *Winter Words* were published in one volume in 1925 as *The Collected Poems* of *Thomas Hardy.* From *The Dynasts* and from Mrs. Florence Emily Hardy's *Early Life of Thomas Hardy* and *Later Years of Thomas Hardy* I have also quoted by permission of Macmillian Co.

To Harper Bros. I am indebted for permission to quote from the following volumes: *Under the Greenwood Tree, The Woodlanders, The Well Beloved, A Laodicean, The Mayor of Casterbridge, Tess of the D'Urbervilles, Two On A Tower, The Return of The Native, Jude The Obscure, Desperate Remedies, A Pair of Blue Eyes, The Trumpet Major, Far From The Madding Crowd, The Hand of Ethelberta, A Group of Noble Dames, Life's Little Ironies, A Changed Man* and *Wessex Tales.*

Other publishers and their editions which I have been permitted to use are as follows: The Living Age Publishing Co., *The Living Age;* William Heineman, Limited, London, *Real Conversations*, by Wm. Archer; The University of Chicago Press, *The Technique of Thomas Hardy*, by J. W. Beach; T. Fisher-Unwin and Ernest Benn, Limited, London, *Thomas Hardy's Universe*, by Ernest Brennecke, Jr.

Chapter I

FOUNDATION OF HARDY'S FATALISM

The further one goes into the works of Thomas Hardy, the more he begins to doubt that the man was a philosopher after all. It is not to be questioned, however, that he had certain consistent, well formed views of life, or that about half way through his life he organized these views into a larger and more comprehensive conception. Yet his entire idea of the Immanent Will seems to have assumed the form of a poetic picture, a graphic set of impressions, forced upon him by his temperament and environment. Certainly, he was primarily an artist and secondarily a philosopher. If this be true, it seems wise to approach and study the motif of fatalism in his works from the point of view of the literary critic rather than from that of the abstract philosopher.

In considering this motif as a product of his random impressions of life, I do not mean to infer that they were not formed from the very beginning by a fundamental idea from which their unity is derived. One is just a little surprised to find that Hardy frequently attempts, with little success, to persuade his readers and critics that his ideas did not possess this unity, and that whatever response and solution his writings furnished to the grave and perplexing questions of life, these solutions were not necessarily his own. In his Preface to *Poems of the Past and Present*, in 1901, he very seriously apologizes for the absence of "cohesion of thought or harmony of colouring" in his works— absolutely the most obvious feature of the book. In an introductory note to *Winter Words*, the last book that he published, he appears at a loss to understand how some of his reviewers could call his *Late Lyrics and Earlier* a gloomy and pessimistic book. "My sense of the oddity of this verdict may be imagined when, in selecting (the poems), I had been, as I thought, rather too liberal in admitting flippant, not to say farcical pieces into the collection." This desire to pose not as a professional philosopher is called attention to by Brennecke, as set forth in the Preface to *The Dynasts*. He says, "Their doctrines", referring to the cosmic comments of his phantom intelligences, or spirits, "are but tentative, and are advanced with but little eye to a systematized philosophy warranted to lift 'the burthen of the mystery' of this unintelligible world."[1] Later in life, when writing a rather contradictory letter to Alfred Noyes, in 1920, he is alarmed that Noyes could find any "belief" in the suitable title, *Time's Laughingstocks*.[2] He repeatedly defended himself against the charge of pessimism which was often brought against him, and in order to combat his critics, invented and added to his system of thought the very clumsy classification, "evolutionary meliorist", which, he says in his Preface to *Late Lyrics and Earlier*, fully describes himself.

It is very easy, I think, to go too far in believing that this was all done deliberately to throw his critics off the trail. No doubt there were connected with the term "pessimism" certain unpleasant connotations which he was not willing to face—especially of intellectual immaturity—associated with it in some prevailing school of thought of the time. Likewise, it appears certain that he was not conscious of the extent to which his interpretation of life and its problems was leading him into the field of pessimism. He was obviously not blind to the truth that his attitude toward these facts differed widely from that held by his Victorian contemporaries and predecessors, but so confident was he in his belief that he was right that he looked upon those who differed with him as if they purposely refused to meet the obvious realities of life. In fact, he was able to conceive of a pessimism more hopeless than his own—a conception which contained no sympathy whatever with human character, no value attached to Goodness, Beauty and Truth for themselves; and feeling this possibility, his attitude, based, as he believed, on his own experience, appeared to him rather lacking in pessimistic content. He says time after time that he has no desire to explain experience; he wishes only to present it. He is merely a fair and impartial judge, whose

---

[1] *Thos. Hardy's Universe*, p. 8
[2] *Later Years*, p. 216

task it is to paint things as he sees them. We get a full expression of this idea in *The Problem*.

> "Shall we conceal the case or tell it—
> We who believe the evidence?"[1]

This idea is carried still further in the Preface to *Poems of The Past and Present*, when Hardy insists that he gives us only "unadjusted impressions" and declares that the "road to a true philosophy of life seems to lie in humbly recording diverse readings of its phenomena as they are forced upon us by chance and change." He was confident that his conception of life was soon destined to be a popular one—one which would be held by generations yet to come. There are numerous evidences of this belief to be found in his works. One case will suffice. He describes Clym Yeobright as one whose face prefigured "the typical countenance of the future", marked with "the view of life as a thing to be put up with", for "what the Greeks only suspected we know well; what their Aeschylus imagined our nursery children feel. That old fashioned revelling in the general situation grows less and less possible as we uncover the effects of natural laws, and see the quandary that man is in by their operation."[2] From this statement we see that Hardy believed that he was treating matters of life just as they were and the charge of pessimism was unfounded. Any other stand on his part would have been taken as a confession that he was giving a warped and distorted account of life. Such a view assumed an encompassing validity in his mind, owing to the fact that throughout his long life he never deemed it necessary to modify his position in any significant way.

Numerous critics have contended that Hardy's gloomy philosophy did not appear in his works until his career was well under way. A careful reading of the novels and poems will not support such a contention. The Folletts, for example, contend that when we look for the element of consistency or continuity in Hardy, we find it in his art, not in his philosophy. The development of his art is a growth, that of his philosophy is a change.[3] It becomes

---

[1] *Collected Poems*, p. 109
[2] *The Return of the Native*, p. 197
[3] *Some Modern Novelists*, p. 128

necessary to show, therefore, that the fundamental basis of the man's fatalism was embodied in his youthful actions and the very first works he wrote, and that there is evidently a gradual development up to the day of his death. It is equally fatuous to contend, I think, as the late Sir Edmund Gosse does, that Hardy "did not budge an inch".[1] There were modifications of a sort, but the basic consistency cannot be questioned.

The basis for this obsession is to be explained by the very temperament of this man of Wessex. In his poem, "The Nightmare and The Next Thing", one catches a glimpse of its uncanny, sadly morbid quality. He discovers nightmares in the very joys of life itself.[2] From his earliest days he possessed a melancholy which he could not shake off. Mrs. Hardy's valuable *Life* records many such impressions.

One of the most essential of these references is one out of his own conversations, an event that "later stood out," he used to say, more vividly than any other single episode in his life. She related that he was flat on his back in the sun, his face covered by an old, torn straw hat, thinking how little he counted for in the world. Meditating on what he had seen and done in the world up to that time, he concluded that he preferred not to grow up.[3] We are told, too, that at this time he was in perfect health and happy circumstances.

His wife also tells how, as a boy, "He loved being alone, but often, to his concealed discomfort, some of the other boys would volunteer to accompany him on his homeward journey to Bockhampton. How much this irked him he recalled long years after."[4] In another connection Mrs. Hardy tells how at sundown, "sitting alone he would recite to himself, 'And now another day is gone', from Dr. Watt's Hymns, with great fervency."[5] From his youth he was violently affected by any kind of calamity. Writing to Rider Haggard in March, 1902, he refers to such a youthful experience: "As a child I knew a sheep-keeping boy who to my horror shortly afterwards died of want—the contents

---

[1] *Edinburgh Review*, vol. 227, p. 284
[2] *Winter Words*, p. 74
[3] *Early Life*, p. 19
[4] *Early Life*, p. 32
[5] *Early Life*, p. 19

of his stomach at the autopsy being raw turnip only."[1] This feeling of his childhood seems to have remained with him to the end. Never in his entire life did he look upon existence as being much worth while. He was the victim of inherent gloom.

For such an unusually sensitive nature, the circumstances of his youth served as an intensifying force to the natural bent of his mind. There appears to be a peculiar significance in the fact that when the poet was born, the attending surgeon thought he was dead. Mrs. Hardy relates it in the following way: "Had it not been for the common sense of the estimable woman who attended as the monthly nurse, he might never have walked the earth. He was thrown aside as dead till rescued by her as she exclaimed to the surgeon, "Dead! Stop a minute! he's alive enough, sure."[2] A frail and rather sickly constitution was his fate throughout his entire life.

He grew increasingly susceptible to the influence of dance music. His wife says that certain dance tunes "always moved the child to tears, though he strenuously tried to hide them . . . This peculiarity in himself troubled the mind of 'Tommy', as he was called, and set him wondering at a phenomenon to which he ventured not to confess. He used to say in later life that like Calantha in Ford's *Broken Heart*, he danced on at these times to conceal his weeping. He was not over four years of age at this date."[3]

Hardy's tender sympathy with nature and his belief in her as an instrument of Fate, which was to become the propelling theme in all of his works, is to be explained by the fact that his entire childhood was spent close to the soil. He was in every sense a child of the Wessex Country. In that small village only a few miles from his beloved Dorchester near the desolate heath of Egdon, we get a glimpse of his lonely boyhood. So very near to nature, he could carefully observe the relentless regularity of natural changes—the more impressive in contrast with the timelessness in the powerful sweep of Nature herself which Egdon Heath symbolized. Funereal wrecks of the past stared

---

[1]*Later Years*, p. 93
[2]*Early Life*, p. 18
[3]*Early Life*, p. 18-19

at the boy on every side—wrecks which lay beyond the amphitheatre at Casterbridge and the old fortress in "A Tryst at an Ancient Earthwork."[1] Such ordinary calamities as poverty and neglect, to which our poet fortunately was never subjected, could not have influenced his temperament toward sorrow and melancholy as did this barren Egdon environment. The fact, too, that he was near the last of an ancient line must have impressed him. Of four children he was the oldest; he was the only one who ever married, and he died childless. In all of this he no doubt saw a symbol of decay. The past glories of his family held an absorbing interest for him as long as he lived. He went so far as to make one of his collateral ancestors, Admiral Sir Thos. Hardy, an associate of the great Lord Nelson and gave him an important role in *The Dynasts*.

A further expression of this youthful melancholy is found in the poem, "He Never Expected Much". The subscription, "(*A Reflection*) *On My Eighty-Sixth Birthday*", leaves no doubt of its personal application. I quote the first and last stanzas only:

> "Well, World, you have kept faith with me,
>   Kept faith with me;
> Upon the whole you have proved to be
>   Much as you said you were.
> Since as a child I used to lie
>   Upon the leaze and watch the sky,
> Never, I own, expected I
>   That life would all be fair . . .
>
> "I do not promise overmuch
>   Child; overmuch;
> Just neutral-tinted haps and such,
>   You said to minds like mine.
> Wise warning for your credit's sake!
> Which I for one failed not to take,
> And hence could stem such strain and ache
>   As each year might assign."[2]

These lines are significant for three reasons: they define the melancholy nature of his childhood; they suggest that his stoically borne life was a record of unhappiness, in spite of the outer appear-

---

[1] *A Changed Man*
[2] *Winter Words*, p. 113-114

ance of contentment; and they show that he thought that Fate ever maintains a disinterested attitude toward man.

Later in life Hardy made efforts to deny the testimony of these poems as to his gloomy outlook on life. In a letter to Alfred Noyes he insists that the following lines from "A Young Man's Epigram on Existence", dated 1866, were written "merely as an amusing instance of early cynicism."[1]

> "A senseless school, where we must give
> Our lives that we may learn to live
> A dolt is he who memorizes
> Lessons that leave no time for prizes."[2]

It is hard to believe that the author of these lines is amused as he says he is, for the regular and insistent recurrence of cynicism in works of his early period convinces us that his statement to Noyes was made lightly or that his memory was very poor.

Moreover, his friends give ample testimony to his peculiar hypochondria. One of the most important statements of this kind is that of T. P. O'Connor: "He was born melancholy, and he remained melancholy throughout his life." Dining with O'Connor, Hardy once remarked, "I didn't think there was anybody in the world that could be so depressed as I can be." O'Connor says significantly that the first Mrs. Hardy was always unsympathetic and unencouraging. "Her whole bitter purpose seemed to be to discourage and belittle and irritate him."[3]

This last statement of O'Connor's perhaps goes far toward explaining Hardy's harsh pictures of womankind. His life with his first wife had been one of incompatibility in temperament and ideals. Just how far apart husband and wife were she innocently tells in her autobiographical record, completed in 1911, a year prior to her death. She concludes by expressing a pious faith in a religion which her husband had long since discarded. She writes: "I have had various experiences, interesting some, sad others, since that lovely day, but all showing that an Unseen Power of great benevolence directs my ways; I have some phil-

[1]*Later Years*, p. 217
[2]*Collected Poems*, p. 281
[3]*Living Age*, vol. 334, 454-6

osophy, and mysticism, and an ardent belief in Christianity and the life beyond this present one, all which makes any existence curiously interesting. As one watches happenings (and even if should occur unhappy happenings), outward circumstances are of less importance if Christ is our highest ideal. A strange unearthly brilliance shines around our path, penetrating and dispersing difficulties with its warmth and glow."[1]

Hardy's early struggle with religious problems was an important factor in shaping his melancholy nature. As early as 1856, he, as a youth of sixteen, was a student of architecture with John Hicks in Dorchester. His fellow pupil, a Baptist, one Bastow, was a very orthodox kind of youth and decided to be baptized. This decision impressed Hardy deeply, and he almost resolved to be baptized also. "He went to the vicar of his parish and stated the case. The vicar, an Oxford man, seemed bewildered, and said that the only book he possessed that might help Hardy was Hooker's *Ecclesiastical Polity*, which he lent his inquirer. Finding that this learned work did not help much in the peculiar circumstances, Hardy went to the curate of another parish with whom he was acquainted. But all that the curate had was an elementary handbook on the Sacraments. However, he got hold of as many books and notes on Paedo-baptism as he could, and though he was appalled at the feebleness of the arguments for infant christening (assuming that New Testament practice must be followed), he incontinently determined to 'stick to his own side', as he considered the Church to be, at some cost of conscience."[2]

Other signs of Hardy's orthodox theism are recorded by Mrs. Hardy. She relates his resentment, as he grew older, of charges of atheism and infidelism hurled at him by critics. She says, "As a child, to be a parson had been his dream; moreover, he had had several clerical relatives who held livings; while his grandfather, father, uncle, brother, wife, cousin, and two sisters had been musicians in various churches over a period covering altogether more than a hundred years. He himself had frequently read the church lessons, and had at one time as a young man

---

[1] *Early Life*, p. 96
[2] *Early Life*, p. 38

begun reading for Cambridge with a view to taking Orders."[1] This last intention "fell through less because of its difficulty than from a conscientious feeling, after some theological study, that he could hardly take the step with honour while holding the views which on examination he found himself to hold."[2]

A painful and grievous process was this loss of religious belief for Hardy, and it was accompanied by deep struggles. In a conversation recorded by William Archer in February, 1901, we get a glimpse of what it all meant to him. He remarked, "I am most anxious to believe in what, roughly speaking, we may call the supernatural—but I find no evidence for it! People accuse me of skepticism, materialism, and so forth; but, if the accusation is just at all, it is quite against my will. For instance, I seriously assure you that I would give ten years of my life—well, perhaps that offer is rather beyond my means—but when I was a young man I would cheerfully have given ten years of my life to see a ghost—an authentic, indubitable spectre."[3] Earlier than this, January 29, 1890, Hardy wrote in his Journal, "I have been looking for God fifty years, and I think if he had existed I should have discovered him. As an external personality, of course—the only true meaning of the word."[4]

In an undated poem, "The Impercipient", published in the first volume of his poetical works (1898), one observes a still more impassioned account of his reluctance to desert orthodox Christianity. He is attending a cathedral service and the first two stanzas, which I quote, represent his mental reaction to this rite:

> "That with this bright believing band
>   I have no claim to be,
> That faiths by which my comrades stand
>   Seem fantasies to me,
> And mirage—mists their Shining Land,
>   Is a strange destiny.

---

[1] *Later Years, p. 176*
[2] *Early Life*, p. 66
[3] *Real Conversations*, p. 37
[4] *Early Life*, p. 293

"Why thus my soul should be consigned
    To infelicity,
Why always I must feel as blind
    To sights my brethren see,
Why joys they've found I cannot find
    Abides a mystery."[1]

It was not a fickle doubt of specific dogma, but an honest questioning of the entire conception of a benevolent God, which caused Hardy to forsake Christianity. It came about as a result of his own observation, aided obviously by his inherently gloomy temperament. It was too much for him to reconcile the idea of beneficence in an omnipotent and omniscient diety with the fact of omnipresent evil and the persistent tendency of circumstances toward the unhappiness of human beings. What mockery to call the ruler over this universal catastrophe "God", an unseen thing to be bowed down to and worshipped! Man's noblest aims and desires for happiness, when pitted against the war of chance, make freedom of individual wills and responsibility for sin farcical interpretations. In the clutches of circumstance, men become puppets, Hamlets, a conception by which Christianity is automatically ruled out.

In spite of this firm attitude toward religious faith, Hardy never became hostile to those who practiced it faithfully. Until his death he hoped that they might change to independent thinking by deserting their thread-bare dogma. This hope is expressed by him in January, 1907, in an article in which he spoke of himself as "the would-be-Religious". "Many millions of the most thoughtful people in England are prevented from entering any church or chapel from year's end to year's end. The days of creeds are as dead and done with as the days of Pterodactyls." As a substitution for them we need "services at which there are no affirmations and no supplications." "In its modern sense" (religion should be merely) "expressive of nobler feelings toward humanity and emotional goodness and greatness, the old meaning of the word—ceremony, or ritual—having perished, or nearly." He then sums up—and here is perhaps the finest touch of religious gloom in his entire works—by saying, "We enter church, and

---

[1] *Collected Poems*, p. 59

we have to say, 'We have erred and strayed from Thy ways like lost sheep', when what we want to say is, 'Why are we made to err and stray like lost sheep?' Then we have to sing, 'My soul doth magnify the Lord', when what we want to sing is, 'O that my soul could find some Lord that it could magnify.' Till it can, let us magnify good works, and develop all means of easing mortals' progress through a world not worthy of them."[1]

Throughout his life he insisted that the liturgy of the church be reformed and revised, and brought into closer harmony with modern thought. This desire was uppermost with him as late as 1925. "Hardy was interested in conjectures on rationalizing the English Church. There had been rumours for some years of a revised Liturgy, and his hopes were accordingly raised by the thought of making the Established Church comprehensive enough to include the majority of thinkers of the previous hundred years who had lost all belief in the supernatural. When the New Prayer Book appeared, however, his hopes were doomed to disappointment, and he found that the revision had not been in a rationalistic direction, and from that time he lost all expectation of seeing the Church representative of modern thinking minds."[2]

Hardy was correct in his objections to charges of atheism. It is not easy to deny that he was an agnostic; yet behind the universe there was an all moving power which he personified as an Immanent Will. His conception of this Power changed at times, yet there is no doubt that he saw it steadily. He makes no effort to force this idea on his fellowmen, but he does insist that the churches do something to fall in line with modern life unless they wish their influence to be lost on an unstable world. His final break with the church of his youth was to leave its clear mark on his temperament. It contributed significantly to that innate pessimism discerned in his nature.

Hardy's works themselves are sufficient evidence that this peculiar turn of temperament persisted and deepened throughout his long life, but even more definite references to it appear in his journal notes. In an entry of November 17-19, 1885, he writes:

[1]*Later Years*, p. 121-122
[2]*Later Years*, p. 225

"In a fit of depression, as if enveloped in a leaden cloud."[1] A few years later he declares that life holds no values for him, and that death is his only hope of escape: "I have attempted many modes (of finding the value of life). For my part, if there is any way of getting a melancholy satisfaction out of life, it lies in dying, so to speak, before one is out of the flesh, by which I mean putting on the manners of ghosts, wandering in their haunts and taking their views of surrounding things. To think of life as passing away is sadness; to think of it as past is at least tolerable. Hence even when I enter into a room to pay a simple morning call I have unconsciously the habit of regarding the scene as if I were a spectre not solid enough to influence my environment; only fit to behold and say, as another spectre said: 'Peace be unto you!'"[2] Such hopeless melancholy as this statement contains will horrify those Hardy readers who feel contented, for there can be no doubt that his hypochondria was a congenital abnormality, terrifying in its ruthlessness. It is here, I think, that we must expect to find the basic germ of that fatalistic philosophy which characterizes almost every novel and poem that he wrote.

This view of life was caused by various external forces. One of these was the period in which Hardy lived. It is now so convenient to dwell upon the foolish optimism of the age of Victoria and the stupid hostility with which many critics and reviewers received his novels, that there is danger of forgetting how thoroughly in harmony Hardy was with one, and the most important thought of the day. He became a prophet to the Victorian Age because he was its product. The prevailing philosophy of the last half of the nineteenth century tended toward a complete condemnation of man's littleness, inherited from the evolutionary discoveries of Spencer and Darwin as they were soon popularized by Huxley. All the time there lay behind its superficial optimism a growing sense of horror, from which timid souls shrank into the relatively secure and unquestioning confines of the church. In literature, this recoil took the form of a renewed and defiant, though somewhat anemic, outburst of the Romantic spirit. Just

---

[1]*Early Life*, p. 230
[2]*Early Life*, p. 275

as the earlier Romantic movement had been a reaction against scientific ideas, or rather against the mechanistic ideas to which the development of mathematical and physical theory gave rise, so the whole Decadent School, especially the Aestheticists, in fear and dissatisfaction, retreated from the mechanistic ideal to which the biological discoveries of their time threatened to lead them. There was something terrifying to them in reducing man from the heroic figure they had once been led to suppose him to be to the puny rank of highest of the animals.

Hardy too felt the implications in these theories, but his courage and the fatalistic sadness of his temperament led him to accept them frankly and almost triumphantly. Disillusion became the refrain of his books, and he actually made a virtue of necessity, constructing works of great beauty on a tragic interpretation of life which to many of his contemporaries was essentially repugnant and to be evaded by a retreat from reality. From this point of view Hardy spoke truly to his age when he entreated it to face things as he saw them. His critics were enraged because he painted in bold colors conditions which they found so frightening that they hid their eyes. He lived into an age that began to doubt whether acceptance of Darwin's theories involved the necessary acceptance of a mechanical universe, but, as one would expect, he could not at that late day revise an outlook to which his temperament predisposed him. The post-war period significantly brought back a revival of that hopelessness of the mechanistic teaching, and consequently a revival of interest in Hardy and his works.

Hardy was confronted with the same problems as his contemporaries were, but he met these issues more courageously than they did. He seized these scientific facts and turned them to imaginative uses, and there is little doubt that his ideas of Nature and the Immanent Will were influenced by them. In this way he embodied the implications of science in one of his chief artistic motifs.

From his youth he was also influenced by that growing distrust of useless social codes which was spread so widely through the plays of Ibsen, Pinero, Wilde and their school. In the chapter on "Convention" this motif will be treated fully. It is necessary to stop here, however, and notice that first and never published novel of Hardy's, *The Poor Man and The Lady*.[1] This work was such a bitter attack on the society of the day that it is surpassed only by *Jude the Obscure*. No doubt he was following a piece of his own advice which he wrote into his essay on "The Profitable Reading of Fiction," that much good is often defeated by too much preaching. "The story", says Mrs. Hardy, "was, in fact, a sweeping dramatic satire of the squire-archy and nobility, London society, the vulgarity of the middle class, modern Christianity, Church restoration, and political and domestic morals in general, the author's views, in fact, being obviously those of a young man with a passion for reforming the world—those of many a young man before and after him; the tendency of the writing being socialistic, not to say revolutionary."[2]

Quite as important was the influence of Hardy's reading, although I cannot help feeling that there has been in recent years a tendency to exaggerate its part in forming a philosophy to which he had gravitated of his own accord. That frantic search for sources and parallels which characterizes one school of criticism has here magnified his borrowings from other thinkers out of true proportion to fact, and incidentally has made him seem responsible for a system of thought far more elaborate and self-conscious than he ever intended it to be. Yet Ernest Brennecke's work on *Thomas Hardy's Universe* and its relation to Schopenhauer's is a very thorough treatment of its subject, which relieves this study of the task of considering in other than a summary way Hardy's philosophy apart from its artistic uses. It must be remembered, however, that his acquaintance with Schopenhauer dates from a period considerably later than that in which the foundations of his view of life were established.

Of Hardy's reading the most significant appear to have been those Greek tragedies which he read as a boy in his early years while working with Hicks in Dorchester.[3] He does not appear to have been concerned with mastering Greek drama at this time, but was content, through press of his work as an architect, with

---

[1] *Early Life*, p. 81
[2] *Early Life* p. 81
[3] *Early Life* p. 43

translating the *Agamemnon* into English. Both W. L. Courtney and A. P. Valakis have considered the relation of Hardy's conception of Fate to that of Aeschylus, a connection which has been far too glibly asserted on other occasions without attempt at a complete understanding of the views of both writers.

According to the belief of the Greeks, the gods were fundamentally opposed to human perfection, because they were jealous of human happiness. These gods were superior to mankind, yet they possessed human characteristics and imperfections, and resented any usurpation of their prerogatives. This attitude of the gods caused all but the stoutest hearted to bow in complete resignation as the wisest course in the face of such hostility. To a certain extent Aeschylus accepted this idea of the gods, but most of his characters belong to that group which refused to be a prey to the whims of the rulers. Prometheus is the supreme example of this independent spirit. Such arrogance on the part of man infuriates the gods, but Aeschylus believes that there is a Fate above both gods and man—a Destiny over which the great Zeus himself has no control. If man has a just complaint against the gods, this Power may aid him, for its chief function is to mete punishments and rewards as they are deserved. Man does, at least, have a measure of free will against this Power, for it takes account of motive and character in its judgments. The Greek free will, then was not necessarily doomed, for by a correct method of living, man might escape annihilation, and not become a mere puppet in the hands of the gods, or fate.

This conception of a just Fate has no parallel in Hardy's Immanent Will, which, whether antagonistic or neutral—and he was never quite able to say which—certainly is not friendly to man. The only point on which the Greek poet and Hardy agree is that there is a controlling Power in the universe. This Power they present not as philosophers, but rather as artists.

Hardy must have been a close student of philosophy during his last years. Especially does he seem to have read those thinkers with whom he agreed. Among these the most important were Schopenhauer and Hartmann. He informs us that they were among his favorites, and that he agreed with their teachings. In a letter to the "Academy" for May 17, 1902, in which he criticises Maeterlinck's "Apology for Nature", he mentions them in a complimentary light.[1]

William Archer records Hardy's statement to the effect that he was indebted to Hartmann.[2] Writing to Helen Garwood, Hardy admitted his philosophical debt to Schopenhauer through later philosophers, among whom no doubt Hartmann and Haeckel were numbered.[3] It must be remembered, however, that Hartmann's chief work was contemporaneous with Hardy's books, and could have served only to codify impressions already fixed.

Brennecke[4] has objected strongly to Miss Garwood's statement[5] that both Schopenhauer and Hardy conceived of the universe as utterly purposeless. Yet there is much ground for admitting that her interpretation does not overstate the case for one of Hardy's most dominant moods. Like Schopenhauer, he was impressed by the evil and unhappiness in life, and he saw no Overseer concerned with this calamity. So long as the motivating force of this universe is blind, all the machinery of its movement and change must be without goal and in this sense purposeless.

Schopenhauer constructed his system on two conceptions: the world as Idea and the world as Will. As Garwood rightly points out, the first of these—the idea that the world exists in our perception of it, our relation to it, and is thus dependent upon our natures—is barely suggested in Hardy. He is too completely concerned with fact and action to take very kindly to this subjective idealism. His chief contact with the German philosopher is through the second of these ideas: the belief that all the phenomenal world originates in the will to live, an all-inclusive force which unites everything in nature. Unfortunately, it cannot take such a multitude of forms without inviting conflict among its individual parts,—or, better, its manifestations. Herein lie Hardy's conflicting conceptions of Fate in Nature which we shall consider in their proper place: that Pantheistic unity of all natural things, with an attendant sympathy among them, and the curious tendency of Nature at times wilfully to

---

[1]*Life and Art*, p. 131
[2]*Real Conversations*, p. 45
[3]*Thomas Hardy, An Illustration of the Philosophy of Schopenhauer*, p. 11
[4]*Thomas Hardy's Universe*, p. 115
[5]*Op. cit., above*

defeat her creatures' nearest desires through the instruments of her other creatures. The very universality of the Will in Schopenhauer and the inevitability of these conflicts implies the conception of an irrational world, a world in which pain must invariably result from conflict. Need we look further for a parallel to Hardy's system, or a complete explanation of that belief that only death constitutes relief from the pain of life? There can be no doubt that Hardy was strongly influenced by Schopenhauer in constructing his conception of the Immanent Will, and that he pictures for us in a startlingly poetic way the very essence of Schopenhauer's thinking.

Hardy probably got from Hartmann the germ of that corollary for his Immanent Will—the melioristic belief that It may be gradually approaching a consciousness which will eventually reconcile contending elements of the earth. He asks William Archer, "Do you know Hartmann's philosophy of the Unconscious? It suggested to me what seemed almost like a workable theory of the great problem of the origin of evil— though this, of course, is not Hartmann's own theory—namely, that there may be a consciousness, infinitely far off, at the other end of the chain of phenomena, always striving to express itself, and always baffled and blundering, just as the spirits seem to be."[1] Certainly the idea is not Hartmann's; it is Schopenhauer's. Hardy fails to tell Archer that Hartmann extended the idea which Hardy eagerly grasped: a hope that some time the Will would successfully interfere with blind determinism and allow truth and good to prevail. Schopenhauer's idea of optimism is not at all like this. He accepted a kind of immortality for everything, inherent in that it is at one with the timeless Will. Loss of individuality comes to man at death, but he survives in an elementary way in that indestructible matter to which he finally crumbles. In other words, all matter is immortal, because the Will is everlasting. Hartmann's hope appealed to Hardy more than that of Schopenhauer's. So completely did he absorb the idea that he soon considered it to be his own. It is to these

---

[1] *Real Conversations*, p. 45-46

two German thinkers, therefore, that we must look for any parallel
theories of determinism which we hope to find in Hardy.

Hardy was acquainted with other philosophers than those
we have mentioned. In 1914 he disagreed thoroughly with
Nietzsche. "He assumes throughout the great worth intrinsically
of human masterfulness. The universe is to him a perfect machine
which only requires thorough handling to work wonders. He
forgets that the universe is an imperfect machine, and that to
do good with an ill-working instrument requires endless adjust-
ments and compromises."[1] No less severe were his objections to
Bergson's theories.[2] The incompatibility of the two men would
make such a fact obvious. There is much significance in these
two statements, because they completely refute the usual concept
that the trend of Hardy's idea was shaped by the authors he read.
His fundamental philosophy was imbedded in his mind many
years before he read any philosopher. His reading merely served
to confirm his beliefs, not to formulate them.

Before this preliminary chapter comes to a close, why not
let Hardy speak on that never ending question: Was Hardy a
pessimist? I have shown that he resented that classification,
and he was justified in his resentment, for it always implied
depreciation and scorn. Later on, however, he accepted it with
restrictions which he defined. I believe that he was much of a
pessimist—at least in the popular philosophical sense of the term.
It may be that his "meliorism" exempts him from that charge.
But let him speak: "People call me a pessimist; and if it is
pessimistic to think, with Sophocles, that 'not to have been born
is best', then I do not reject the designation. I never could
understand why the word 'pessimism' should be such a red flag
to many worthy people; and I believe that a good deal of the
robustious, swaggering optimism of recent literature is at bottom
cowardly and insincere. I do not see that we are likely to improve
the world by asseverating, however loudly, that black is white,
or at least that black is but a necessary contrast and foil, without
which white would be white no longer. That is mere juggling
with a metaphor. But my pessimism, if pessimism it be, does

---

[1] *Later Years*, p. 160
[2] *Later Years*, pp. 127-8, 270-3

not involve the assumption that the world is going to the dogs, and that Ahriman is winning all along the line. On the contrary, my practical philosophy is distinctly meliorist. What are my books but one long plea against man's inhumanity to man—to woman—and to the lower animals . . . When we have got rid of a thousand remediable ills, it will be time enough to determine whether the ill that is irremediable outweighs the good."[1]

[1]*Real Conversations*, pp. 46-47

CHAPTER II

HARDY'S CONCEPTION OF FATE:
ITS DEVELOPMENT

In both prose and poetry Hardy's work finds its unity in Fate as a central theme. Its rigid monotony of tone and its uncompromising sincerity are, as we have observed, derived from convictions deep seated within the temperament and philosophy of the man himself. But the exact nature of Hardy's conception of Fate has not been defined; it has only been hinted at. In this chapter I wish to attempt such a definition by a study of its development by impressions of his early years down to its culmination in the *Dynasts*.

But before an attempt is made to determine how and why Hardy was a fatalist, our terms must be defined. We cannot agree on a clearer definition of Fatalism than that it is that view of life which insists that all action everywhere is controlled by the nature of things or by a power superior to things. It grants the existence of Fate, "a great impersonal, primitive force, existing from all eternity, absolutely independent of human wills, superior even to any god whom humanity may have invented."[1] The power of this Fate is all embracing, and is more difficult of understanding than the gods themselves. Individual fatalists have held varied conceptions of it, but the fact here stated may be said to apply, in a general way at least, to all of them.

The scientific parallel of fatalism is determinism. It acknowledges, just as does fatalism, that man's struggle against the Will behind things, is of no avail, but it does decree that the laws of cause and effect must not suspend operation. To put it in another way, determinism seeks to explain conditions which fatalism is content to describe.

---

[1]Courtney, W. L. "*Fate and the Tragic Sense. Transactions of the Royal Society of Literature.*" 2nd Series, v. 28, p. 217

The subject matter of this chapter may be better comprehended if I state that I consider Hardy to have been both a fatalist and a determinist. He was neither a scientist nor a philosopher, but an artist with a steady view of life. The fact, therefore, that his mind fluctuated between fatalism and determinism, and at times accepted both, cannot be held as a nullification of his consistency. He was not interested in consistency so far as it concerned a technical distinction between them. He considered both to be mere varied reactions to the same point of view.

Hardy's reading public possessed a very incomplete idea of the philosophy that motivated his work until the appearance of his first volume of poetry in 1898, two years after he stopped novel composition. No doubt, however, could have been held as to its general trend, for *Tess* and *Jude* had given it bitter expression. But for a codification of his ideas in unmistakable form one must turn to his verse. In 1896 he had written, "Perhaps I can express more fully in verse ideas and emotions which run counter to the inert crystallized opinion—hard as rock—which the vast body of men have vested interests in supporting. To cry out in a passionate poem that (for instance) the Supreme Mover of Movers, The Prime Force of Forces, must be either limited in power, unknowing, or cruel—which is obvious enough, and has been for centuries—will cause them merely a shake of the head; but to put it in argumentative prose will make them sneer, or foam, and set all the literary contortionists jumping upon me, a harmless agnostic, as if I were a clamorous atheist, which in their crass illiteracy they seem to think is the same thing."[1] Behind this bitter feeling is the enthusiasm of the crusader, the reformer, through the pages of literature, spreading a doctrine devastating in its hopelessness. His poetry is full of this kind of philosophy.

Though one of the greatest of tragic poets, Hardy is of a peculiar kind. That he himself failed to understand that his tragedies differed in motivation from the accepted standard is indicated in his own statements about the tragic spirit in literature. He wrote that "A Plot, or Tragedy, should arise from gradual closing in of a situation that comes of ordinary human passions, pre-

---

[1] *Later Years*, p. 57-58

judices, and ambitions, by reason of the characters taking no
trouble to ward off the disastrous events produced by the said
passions, prejudices, and ambitions."[1] This statement fits well
the construction of a *Hamlet* or an *Agamemnon*, but does it fit
Tess or *The Woodlanders?* It is not character which is the
controlling factor in Hardy's tragic works, but it is a power beyond
man and deliberately opposed to his will—a power which we
shall, for the moment, call Fate. He is more explicit in another
passage when he says, "Tragedy may be created by an opposing
environment either of things inherent in the universe, or of human
institutions."[2]

Now Hardy's tragedy can be said to spring from within the
human actor only in so far as this universal force fastens one of
its tentacles within the very mind of man. That is to say, not
character, but instinct is able to bring his actors to grief; over
this instinct, however, they possess no more control than they
do over mere Chance, which wrecks their happiness. Hardy
has told us plainly that Jude's tragedy is not that his love experiences failed utterly, but that he failed to consummate his noble
aspirations for an educational and a useful life. In this defeat,
sexual instinct from within was as much his enemy as the uncompromising traditions of Christminster, the narrowness of
convention and the blighting nature of womanhood,—against
all which manifestations of Fate he was mercilessly pitted. Moreover, Fate does not apportion these instincts with an eye for their
appropriateness to the individual's problem or environment,—
or even equally among all human beings. Some of his people
are doomed to be like eunuchs in a harem; others like epicures in
a well stocked cafe. We have no choice but to accept the ill-
assorted hand that is dealt us. "Life is what we make it as
Whist is what we make it; but not as Chess is what we make it;
which ranks higher as a purely intellectual game than Whist or
Life."[3] Often this hand contains some tainted cards from heredity
—that unsuitability to marriage which hangs over Jude's family
like an ominous myth, the more terrible because we see it proved

---

[1] *Early Life*, p. 157
[2] *Later Years*, p. 44
[3] *Later Years*, p. 96

true. Sometimes it is the mark of a foreign race or nation bequeathed by ancestors which estranges his people from their environment. This conflict of the individual temperament with its surroundings of Eustacia Vye with Egdon Heath—is a sure index to unhappiness and tragedy, and sometimes the caprice,— or the malignant determination of Fate delights in burdening his creatures with such an inescapable incompatibility with environment.

Any kind of dogmatic assertion that character is not Fate in Hardy is made void by one salient exception,—Michael Henchard of Casterbridge. Those critics who have determined to coordinate character and Fate in his works, quite naturally turn to this book for proof.[1] The conception of Destiny as held by Aeschylus is more closely approached in *The Mayor of Casterbridge* than any other of our author's works. Henchard's own character and his unethical business methods positively account for his tragic end. No instinctive and unanswerable craving for drink leads him to that dive, where in a partially drunken state he auctions off his wife and brings upon himself lifelong wretchedness. She had been meek and long suffering, and neither her action nor a malignant force outside himself drove him to it. Again his dishonorable attempt to ruin Farfrae was intentional and self-willed, and, with a sense of justice strange in Hardy though typical of Aeschylus, Fate, through the instrument of its weather-god, defeats his aim and brings ruin upon Henchard himself in a deliberate way. Truly "Character is Fate" here, as Hardy quotes from Novalis.

We find it as well in delineation of some of his villains—Troy and Dare, especially, though not D'Urberville, who is burdened with a sensuality against which, in fact his better nature struggles, though unsuccessfully. We sometimes feel that these villains have moulded their own lives to a large extent, and that they deserve the disaster which usually overtakes them. But this is not true of Hardy's characters in general; the evidence is overwhelming on the other side. As he remarks of his Bishop of Manchester, they are far "too good for their destiny."[2] Some-

---

[1]Gardner, *Some Thoughts on the Mayor of Casterbridge* p. 20
[2]*Two on a Tower*, p. 290

times, especially in his early novels, he felt under compulsion to give his plot "a predetermined cheerful ending"[1] but even here we sense an obvious reluctance, a compromise upon peace and joys realized so late that much of their sweetness is lost. This is most noticeable in the marriages at the end of *Far From the Madding Crowd* and *The Woodlanders* which seem not the triumphs of the will to human happiness over great obstacles, but rather mere makeshifts for contentment, in which Fate has no less surely its triumph in the destruction of happy illusion.

The basis of Hardy's fatalistic conception of life lies in that inevitable clash between the human will to enjoy and the Immanent Will to defeat it, or, as he has himself stated it, "the inherent will to enjoy and the circumstantial will against enjoyment!"[2] In this struggle the latter is almost invariably triumphant because it has all of the forces above on its side. There is a significant implication in his using the term "enjoy", for it suggests a fact about Hardy's outlook that must be remembered throughout this discussion. Happiness for him consists of enjoyment of a very concrete and rather obvious kind, a revelling in the actual delights of existence. The source of happiness is not within ourselves, but is dependent on external factors, on securing what we want most in life. Virtue is not really its own reward in Hardy,—the examples of Marty South and Tess notwithstanding. A devotion to truth and goodness can ennoble human nature in struggle and disappointment, but it does not constitute repayment. It may exalt human life, but it does not make it bearable.

This primary concern with the overpowering importance of external things is one of the keynotes of all his art. It is akin to that aspect of his methods of plot construction noticed by Beach: "He seems to have read life in terms of action, of objective action; in terms of brute incident, things happening."[3] Hardy was not aroused primarily by unhappiness around him, but by the tendency of external circumstances to bring it about. This explains why throughout his books psychology is subordinated

---

[1] *Preface to A Laodicean*, p. vii
[2] *Tess of the D'Urbervilles*, p. 327
[3] *The Technique of Thomas Hardy*, p. 12

to incident. When objection is made to the importance of accident and coincidence in Hardy's plots, it must be remembered that these are not merely bungling methods of construction, but purposeful devices born of his way of looking at life. He saw primarily the objective nature of joy and pain and the role played by incident in causing them. On one occasion he wrote, "Art is a changing of the actual proportions and order of things, so as to bring out more forcibly than might otherwise be done that feature in them which appeals most strongly to the idiosyncrasy of the artist . . . Art is a disproportioning of realities, to show more clearly the features that matter in those realities, which, if merely copied or reported inventorially, might possibly be observed, but would more probably be overlooked."[1] From this statement it is obvious that he was concerned with things, realities and happenings. That these very realities are kept moving by an immanent plan that disregards man, is the very essence of his determinism. What can man do when living under such a condemnation? The best plan would appear to be one of resignation and submission, but that brings no relief. Those who submit get exactly the same disaster and sorrow as those who rebel: Eustacia and Wildeve, Marty South and Tess. This power asks and gives no quarter. Hardy seems, however, to prefer those who submit; perhaps this group lives by a higher code than their Maker.

Truth, Beauty and Goodness are always worth cherishing, but only because their opposites are not. In fact, within a man's very goodness may lie his own undoing. Almost every step which brings sorrow to Tess has its origin in a lofty motive. It is due to her desire to aid her parents that she goes to market on that fatal day. A like desire sends her to her fatal position at the D'Urbervilles. In her desire to escape from a group of vulgar women she is thrown into the clutches of Alec D'Urberville. Subsequently, her baby dies of cold and hunger because she, for the sake of honor, refuses the aid Alec offers. Her marriage with Clare is wrecked because by her code of honor she must tell him of her affair with D'Urberville. It often appears that

---

[1] *Early Life*, p. 299

in Hardy's late novels the odds are against virtue. Jude is discharged by his employer for allowing the hungry crows to pick up the grain. From this experience the boy learns of that "flaw in the terrestial scheme, by which what was good for God's birds was bad for God's gardener."[1] Such a revelation for Jude was perhaps sufficient, for it forms the essence of Schopenhauer's idea of conflict of creatures who are but one in the universal Will. If this lesson was grasped by Jude, it was sufficient for an eventful lifetime.

Hardy's resignation often drops into fearful satire, which the poem, "Mad Judy", well illustrates:

> "When the hamlet hailed a birth
> Judy used to cry:
> When she heard our christening mirth
> She would kneel and sigh.
> She was crazed, we knew, and we
> Humored her infirmity . . .
>
> "When old Headsman Death laid hands
> On a babe or twain,
> She would feast, and by her brands
> Sing her songs again.
> What she liked we let her do,
> Judy was insane we knew."[2]

"The Dame of Athelhall" is a good example of loyalty resulting in misery. This poem is an account of a wife who, while eloping with her lover, becomes stricken with remorse, returns to her husband to find that he has taken another for his love and had not regretted her elopement.[3] As a result of her loyalty all four are brought to grief. In "The Turnip-Hoer", again a good act defeats the actor, who rescues a duchess from peril and then turns to drink and death because of a hopeless longing for her.[4]

Throughout much of Hardy's work this tone of irony is evident; when applied to important situations it is usually handled by some kind of frustration. As in "The Dame of Athelhall" and

---

[1] *Jude the Obscure*, p. 11
[2] *Collected Poems*, p. 138
[3] *Collected Poems*, p. 141
[4] *Ibid*, p. 667

other poems like it, this frustration often concerns the happiness of four people. In other cases characters are allowed to realize their wishes only after they have ceased to wish. The "Interlopers at the Knap," (1884) is a good instance of this. Here Sally is heartlessly separated from her lover at the very time of the wedding, and is forced to see him marry another.[1] When he is free to claim her many years later, she refuses him and prefers to live alone. This idea is slightly varied in another Wessex Tale, "The Waiting Supper." Here a capricious girl chooses the wrong suitor and soon regrets it. The jilted lover remains loyal, the husband disappears, but since there is no proof of his death, the two lovers cannot marry. After seventeen long years, they learn that he was drowned on the very night of his disappearance, but not knowing it, they could not profit by it. When marriage is possible, she has lost all desire and they never unite. In this story frustration is caused by misunderstanding, one of Hardy's most frequent and most tantalizing devices.[2]

Another of his pet themes for frustration is seen in this story: the wrecking of chances for subsequent happiness by some act of indiscretion in early life, or a compromising decision made in haste or before maturity. An hour is quite enough time for Henchard to wreck his life at Weydon Priors furmity stand. The few moments spent with Alec on the Chase doom Tess forever. Jude's hasty marriage with Arabella makes a request of Sue's hand impossible, at a time when she might have accepted him. In Jude's case, it is doubtful that happiness lay that way, yet his entire life of misery dates from the moment that Arabella attracted his attention with the pig offal.

Hardy obviously sees the hand of fate in all of these ironical situations, an intentional interference by Destiny in the affairs of men, or a system in which all things tend toward sorrow and irony. This irony is not always tragic, however. Sometimes it is of a humorous type. A case of this is that of Viviette, who, when she discovers that she is to bear Swithin an illegitimate child, marries the unsuspecting Bishop of Manchester, who has just proposed to her. This touch of humor saves the situation

---

[1] Wessex Tales, 1898
[2] *A Changed Man.*

from tragedy.[1] But such interludes in austerity come almost too seldom to count, for they represent Hardy's wanton Fate in a mood of playfulness—a mood rare with the author. In most cases it is purely hostile, set upon robbing man of joy in a most perplexing way. Here is the Wyrd of ancient Wessex in its most deadly form.

Now this conception of Fate was organized through slow years of evolution; and its growth can be traced from the man's early years down to the *Dynasts*. In this process we see an unswerving tendency toward definition.

In Hardy's first poems we see the aftermath of his early religious struggles already referred to. Development begins with these. We first encounter it in an increasing doubt of a purposeful order in the world:

> "(Nature's) loves dependent on a feature's trim,
> A whole life's circumstance on hap of birth,
> A soul's direction on a body's whim,
> Eternal Heaven upon a day of Earth,
> Is frost to flower of heroism and worth,
> And fosterer of visions ghast and grim."[2]

In "The Two Men" the presence of Divine Justice is doubted. One person lives a life of indulgence, another lives a life of denial, yet both reach the same end—poverty and death. But moralists would say that they were alike in all they did.[3] Moreover, present joy is no promise of future happiness, "for winters freeze; for you will tire; for you will fade; for you will die."[4] Hardy would teach us, it seems, that happiness is but a forerunner of grief. In "Revulsion" (1866), in order that he may never know disappointment, he hopes he will never love.[5] Still he is not quite sure that all of this can be charged to a predetermined system. In "Ditty—E. L. G.," (1870), he says that Chance and Hap may be responsible and it annoys him:

---

[1] *Two on a Tower*, Chap. 39
[2] *Collected Poems*, p. 798
[3] *Ibid*, p. 68-70
[4] *Heiress and Architect*, C. P. p. 67
[5] *Collected Poems*, p. 11

"To feel I might have kissed—
Loved as true—
Otherwise, nor Mine have missed
My life through,
Had I never wandered near her,
Is a smart severe—severer
In the thought that she is naught,
Even as I, beyond the dells,
Where she dwells.

"And Devotion droops her glance
To recall
What bondservants of Chance
We are all.
I but found her in that going
On my errant path unknowing,
I did not out-skirt the spot
That no spot on earth excels—
Where she dwells."[1]

Perhaps the closest solution for this terrible condition of affairs is found in the little poem, "Hap." (1866) one of Hardy's first pieces of verse. Here he wishes that the great Mover were deliberately malicious and vengeful. At least man would know what to expect:

"Then would I bear it, clench myself, and die,
Steeled by the sense of ire unmerited;
Half-eased in that a Powerfuller than I
Had willed and meted me the tears I shed.

"But not so. How arrives it joy lies slain,
And why unblooms the best hope ever sown?
—Crass Casualty obstructs the sun and rain,
And dicing Time for gladness casts a moan . . .
These purblind Doomsters had as readily strown
Blisses about my pilgrimage as pain."[2]

The first suggestion of an Immanent Will is to be found in these "purblind Doomsters" of "Hap." They deal out sorrow, not because they choose to do so, but because they are blind and can do no other. Nowhere in Hardy's early writings does he come more closely to an analysis of the nature and source of our

---

[1]*Collected Poems*, p. 14
[2]*Ibid*, p. 7

ills. It is a monistic view: a rule by "Crass Casualty," assisted by Time.

Since we know that Hardy considered verse as a most satisfactory medium for expressing philosophy, we are not surprised to find in *Desperate Remedies*, (1870), his first published novel, a more vague statement. There are definite impressions, but not any system. The religious hope which remained in Hardy and its change to a later explanation of matters is embodied in his statement that "Reasoning worldliness, especially when allied with sensuousness, cannot repress on some extreme occasions the human instinct to pour out the soul to some Being, or Personality, who in frigid moments is dismissed with the title of Chance, or at most,—Law."[1] Already this Personality had taken on a hostile shape. In his confession Manston says that "Providence, whom I had just thanked, seemed a mocking tormentor laughing at me."[2] It is perhaps a little odd that we discover in the rustics of Hardy a clearer idea of Fate than we do in his better actors. No doubt this is true because they are nearer the soil and more akin to the spirit of the Wessex Wyrd. In the following lines the two classes appear to have merged their fatalism into a kind of deity. The maid and the clerk are conversing: "God A'mighty," says she, "always sends bread as well as children." He answers: "But 'tis the bread to one house and the children to another very often."[3] Then too, these rustics appear more resigned to their fate than their superiors, but none escapes its influence. Cytherea comments: "Is it the intention of Fate that something connected with these noises should influence my future as in the last case of the kind?"[4]

The element of Fate is subordinated to a greater degree than anywhere else in that romantic tale *Under the Greenwood Tree*, (1872). It is unique in many ways. The idea of woman as an instrument of Fate in annoying man forms its chief contact with the growth of Hardy's fatalistic conception. The theme of rustic resignation to Fate of *Desperate Remedies* is retained here,

---

[1]*Desperate Remedies*, p. 210
[2]*Ibid*, p. 433
[3]*Desperate Remedies*, p. 273
[4]*Ibid*, p. 268

too. Mr. Penny says of ill luck: " 'Twas to be, and none can gainsay it.' "[1] The tranter says later, " 'Ay, your pa'son comes by fate: 'tis heads or tails, like pitch-halfpenny, and no choosing; so we must taken en as he is, my sonnies, and thank God he's no worse, I suppose."[2]

The crystallization of this conception sees a great advance in *A Pair of Blue Eyes*, (1873). Hardy still has Chance and Determinism in his thoughts, and had, at this time, made no choice between them. He was so little concerned with their distinction that he saw no conflict between them. The story contains an almost incredible number of coincidences; at times Hardy appears to doubt that Chance is always to blame. "Strange conjunctions of circumstance, particularly those of a trivial everyday kind, are so frequent in an ordinary life, that we grow used to their unaccountableness, and forget the question whether the very long odds against such juxtaposition is not almost a disproof of its being a matter of chance at all." The actors in the story, early as it is, seem to feel and shun the presence of Fate everywhere. Elfride will not give her lover a lock of her hair, because she believes it bad luck.[3] The maturing of Hardy's philosophy begins with this remarkable novel.[4]

Chance gives place to determinism still more in *Far from the Madding Crowd*, (1874). Fate is strong in such coincidences as Fanny Robin's mistaking All Souls Church for All Saints, an error sufficient to wreck three lives completely and postpone the joy of two more.

In *The Return of the Native*, (1878), we notice the development of this idea still further. Here are many "cruel satires that Fate loves to indulge in."[5] This is the first of his novels in which Fate seems fully grown. The development of the idea of the influence of Nature on the actions of Egdon Heath people is obvious, but there is another aspect of the conception: that realization of Fate within the characters themselves, an idea that is to reach its climax in Napoleon's sense of relation with

[1]*Under the Greenwood Tree*, p. 12
[2]*Ibid*, p. 91
[3]*R. A. Firor—Folkways in Thomas Hardy*
[4]*To be treated in Chapter III*
[5]*Return of the Native*, p. 243

the Immanent Will in *The Dynasts*. The character in *The
Native* who is the whim of Fate is Eustacia Vye, the revolting
spirit of the Heath.   She, by her horror of poverty, can see further
into its sources than her friends.   Hardy says of her, "She can
show a most reproachful look at times, but it was directed less
against human beings than against certain creatures of her mind,
the chief of these being Destiny, through whose interference she
dimly fancied it arose that love alighted only on gliding youth—
that any love she might win would sink simultaneously with the
sand in the glass."[1]   Instead of blaming herself when Clym's
mother is turned from his door, Eustacia blames some colossal
Prince of the World.[2]   Realizing that she cannot escape, she
weeps bitterly: "How I have tried and tried to be a splendid
woman, and how destiny has been against me!   I do not deserve
my lot!   O, the cruelty of putting me into this ill-conceived
world!   I was capable of much; but I have been injured and
blighted and crushed by things beyond my control!   O, how hard
it is of Heaven to devise such torture for me, who have done no
harm to Heaven at all."[3]

Wildeve, also, has a vague belief in Fate: "The fates have
not been kind to you, Eustacia Yeobright", he says, and she
answers: "I have nothing to thank them for."[4]   One would
hardly expect the hopeful Clym Yeobright to believe in Fate;
yet even he does so, though with reluctance.   Hardy says of
him, "he did sometimes think he had been ill-used by fortune
so far as to say that to be born is a palpable dilemma, and that
instead of men aiming to advance in life with glory they should
calculate how to retreat out of it without shame . . . yet, human
beings, in their generous endeavor to construct an hypothesis
that shall not degrade a first Cause, have always hesitated to
conceive a dominant power of lower moral quality than their
own."[5]   Clym, in complete resignation adds, " 'Well, what
must be, will be.' "   His feeling is that acquiescence in fatalism
that comes after abject failure.

---

[1] *Return of the Native*, p. 79
[2] *Ibid*, p. 353
[3] *Ibid*, p. 422
[4] *Ibid*, p. 334
[5] *Ibid*, p. 455

By the time Hardy wrote the *Return of the Native* the idea of
Fate was so completely dominating his novels that it appears
even in his less serious moments. There is a little comedy of
"The Distracted Preacher," (1879) in which there is a "young
fellow," doomed to suffer at the hands of a woman.[1] In another
Wessex Tale, "The Fellow Townsmen" (1880), we read that
"events that had, as it were, dashed themselves together in one
half hour of this day showed that curious refinement of cruelty
in their arrangement which often proceeds from the bosom of
the whimsical god at other times known as blind Circumstance."[2]
In these tales the actors seem to be conscious of the power beyond
themselves. One says, "I suppose it was destiny-accident-
I don't know what, that separated us, dear Lucy." Another
adds: "The Fates have rather ill used me." Through calam-
itous misunderstanding Fate gets in its work in "What the Shepherd Saw," (1881). Ogbourne is killed by the Duke, because
he was so far off that he could not hear the conversation which he,
the Duke, took to be a guilty one between the fellow and his wife.[3]
    In a general way this development is observed in that dullest
and, I think, the worst of the novels, *A Laodicean.* (1882).   There
is a "star"[4] which directs Somerset, and it is obvious that each
person in the story has a "star" also. The heroine Paula "felt
that Providence had stepped in to shape ends that she was too
undecided or unpractised to shape for herself."[5] DeStancy,
with more resignation, says, "Well let it be, it cannot be
helped; destiny is supreme."[6]   Sir William   has   more
definite ideas on the subject: "Not that I mean to say
that luck lies in any one place long, or at any one person's doors.
Fortune likes new faces, and your wisdom lies in bringing your
acquisitions into safety, while her favour lasts."[7]   In *Two on a
Tower* the Bishop humiliates his dignity" with the air of a man
too good for his destiny—which, to be just to him, was not far

---

[1] *Wessex Tales*
[2] *Ibid*, 155
[3] *A Changed Man*, p. 187
[4] *A Laodicean*, p. 288
[5] *Ibid*, p. 233
[6] *Ibid*, p. 434
[7] *Ibid*, p. 52

from the truth."[1]   Chance is evident in "The Romantic Adventures of a Milkmaid" 1883.   The Baron says, "There seems to be a fate in all this; I get out of the frying pan into the fire."[2] We are advised in "A Mere Interlude," (1885), that "it would be as well to take what fate offered."[3]   I have considered thus briefly those minor stories with which Hardy was busy in that seven-year period after *The Return of the Native*.   While they show his fatalistic trend, they do not show its crystallization.

We have observed that *The Mayor of Casterbridge*, in which "Character is Fate," interrupts the growth of Hardy's conceptions. The system into which his views were fitting left no place for character, because such an admission would necessarily postulate free will and divine Justice,—two things which did not exist for him.   He does allow Henchard free will, but the end is so tragic that its desirability is nullified.   Fate still has its clutches on the Mayor, but it is Fate of the Aeschylean brand rather than that of Hardy.   He may choose safety or destruction; he chooses the latter, and Fate deals the reward.   But this choice is perhaps better than no choice at all.   Therefore, this novel kindles a little ray of hope that perhaps happier things are ahead in Hardy, but suddenly that hope is fanned completely out.

It is strange that in this novel Hardy was at so much pains to make his actors completely conscious of the existence of Fate. Henchard knows it and blames it for a great many of his sins. His wife "plodded on in the shade of the hedge, silently thinking; she had the hard, half-apathetic expression of one who deems anything possible at the hands of Time and Chance, except, perhaps, fair play."[4]   Her words were "in the resigned tone of a fatalist."[5]   Farfrae belongs to the fatalistic type of Aeschylus. He can conceive of some good issuing from a Divine Power. After he is chosen Mayor, he says, "See now how it's ourselves that are ruled by the power above us!   We plan this, but we do that."[6]

---

[1] *Two on a Tower*, p. 290
[2] *A Changed Man*, p. 355
[3] *Ibid*, p. 265
[4] *The Mayor of Casterbridge*, p. 2
[5] *Ibid*, p. 17
[6] *Ibid*, p. 280

Elizabeth Jane's sorrow had left its mark on her. Hardy says, "She had still that field-mouse fear of the coulter of destiny despite fair promise, which is common among the thoughtful who have suffered early from poverty and oppression. 'I won't be too gay on any account', she would say to herself! 'It would be tempting Providence to hurl Mother and me down, and afflict us again as he used to do'."[1]   In this novel Hardy returns to a favorite trick of his, already mentioned, of having Fate resort to substitution rather than complete disappointment. "She had learnt the lesson of renunciation, and was as familiar with the wreck of each day's wishes as with the diurnal setting of the sun. If her earthly career had taught her few book philosophies, it had at least well practised her in this.   Yet her experience had consisted less in a series of pure disappointments than in a series of substitutions.   Continually it had happened that what she had desired had not been granted her and what had been granted her she had not desired.   So she viewed with an approach to equanimity the now cancelled days when Donald had been her undeclared lover, and wondered what unwished-for-thing Heaven might send her in place of him."[2]   Her views were correct, for she too, had her "malignant star."   Her experiences had taught her that "happiness was but the occasional episode in a general drama of pain."[3]

A definite return to a complete determinism is represented by *The Woodlanders*, 1887.   What he had formerly called "Chance" is no longer a haphazard thing, but the manifestation of an unrelenting Fate.   In this novel there is an event for every cause, yet there is in human will and character no bases for that cause. The cause is the resultant of an Immanent Will, over which man has no control.   That host of incidents and accidents that aided in spoiling Giles's carefully prepared dinner had their own cause, yet Giles was helpless to prevent them.   No wonder the poor fellow felt "that the fates were against him."[4]

Hardy's fatalistic philosophy finds its supreme and final prose

---

[1] *The Mayor of Casterbridge*, p. 101
[2] *Ibid*, p. 205
[3] *Ibid*, p. 386
[4] *The Woodlanders*, p. 73

expression in *Tess of the D'Urbervilles*, 1891, and *Jude the Obscure*, 1896. The progress from ungoverned Chance to cruel determinism, as well as all of the other phases of his philosophy which we have considered, are in these two tragedies united in a positive way. His fatalism, for the most part, up to the time of *Tess*, can be explained on the basis of temperament alone and such melancholy as is found in many of his characters. But *Tess* and *Jude* give us an entirely different problem; the immortals are united; they have elected a President and man is faced with a system.

Notice that in *Tess* Hardy applies the word "fatalism" to his own idea of things. Near the start of the story he bids us lament for the tragedy of his heroine and says, "As Tess's own people down in those retreats are never tired of saying among each other in their fatalistic way: 'It was to be! There lay the pity of it.'"[1] Further on he adds, "in the lonely country nooks, fatalism is a strong sentiment."[2] To a greater extent than ever before, persistent fatalism is reflected in his actors of *Tess*. For instance, it motivates all that Tess's mother does. The death of the horse, the knowledge of Tess's ill-luck with Alec, even the failure of her marriage with Clare, her mother accepts as though some high and uncompromising hand is dealing out these disappointments. When her mother hears of the wrecked marriage, Hardy says, "After her first burst of disappointment, Joan began to take the mishap as she had taken Tess's original trouble, as she would have taken a wet holiday or a failure of the potato crop."[3] Alec is a victim of this same feeling, but it takes a different turn: "that reckless acquiescence in change too apparent in the whole D'Urberville family."[4] Tess's milkmaid friend, Marian, after Clare had gone, said to Tess: "You've no faults, deary; that I'm sure of. And he's none. So it must be something outside ye both."[5] But above all other characters of the story Tess herself is the fullest expression of fatalism. She, from the beginning, is hopelessly resigned to her doom. "The honesty, directness,

---

[1] *Tess*, p. 80
[2] *Tess*, p. 163
[3] *Tess*, p. 293
[4] *Ibid*, p. 289
[5] *Ibid*, p. 323

and impartiality of elemental enmity disconcerted her but little."[1]
Tess found comfort in ignorance, and refuge in blindly refusing
to know the worst. She puts it clearly: "Because what's the
use of learning that I am one of a long row only finding out that
there is set down in some old book somebody just like me, and
to know that I shall only act her part; making me sad, that's
all. The best is not to remember that your nature and your
past doings have been just like thousands' and thousands'."[2]
But she still was not sure of her refuge and illusions. Happiness,
she thought, "may be scourged out of me afterward by a lot of
ill. That's how God mostly does."[3] Her consciousness of her
own innocent life makes her doom all the more tragic. "Never
in her life—she could swear it from the bottom of her soul—had
she intended to do wrong; yet these hard judgments had come.
Whatever her sins, they were not sins of intention, but of inad-
vertence, and why should she have been punished so persistent-
ly?"[4] No wonder she longed for death! "Sheer experience had
already taught her that, in some circumstances, there was one
thing better than to lead a good life, and that was to be saved
from leading any life whatever. Like all who had been previs-
ioned by suffering, she could, in the words of M. Sully—Prud-
homme, hear a penal sentence in the fiat, 'You shall be born,'
particularly if addressed to potential issue of hers."[5] Everywhere in Hardy's people resignation is so manifest that often
there appears to be no conflict at all—no material for any kind
of tragedy or drama. Still there is a subtler kind of tragedy. Tess
and Jude, though resigned to the inevitability of Fate, still retain
a will to live and enjoy. It is true, the odds are stacked against
them, but the conflict is there.

The case of Jude is just as hopeless as that of Tess. Fate is
against him in full force. Heredity, (for the Fawley family had
never been happy in wedlock), coincidence, woman, convention,
and every other tool known to Fate is brought to play upon his
pitiful soul. Most pathetic of all is that he should possess such

[1]*Tess*, p. 320
[2]*Ibid*, p. 141
[3]*Ibid*, p. 234
[4]*Tess*, p. 409
[5]*Ibid*, p. 277

an abnormally sensitive nature. This fact causes his defeats at the hands of Fate to be especially tragic—more so than they could be to a more rugged person. His nature predisposes him to a sorrowful life.

We feel the pain of this tragedy all the more because we know that Jude did nothing to bring it about. Tess sinned, innocently it is true, but it was sin withal. He was kind and tender to all living things. He is discharged from his first position because he felt too kindly toward some crows and wanted them to have food. This result astounds him; "Nature's logic was too horrid for him to care for."[1] More significant is the repulsive episode of the pig-killing. "The white snow, stained with the blood of his fellow mortal, wore an illogical look to Jude as a lover of Justice, not to say a Christian."[2] Then there is his extreme pain at seeing a rabbit caught in a trap.[3] Jude's loyalty is little less attractive than his sympathy. He cannot forget his old schoolmaster, Phillotson, and longs to see him once more. When he does see him, Phillotson has completely forgotten him. Later on, this devotion of Jude's is to be repaid by Phillotson's robbing him of Sue. In Jude's mind the sense of duty has highly developed. He complied with Arabella's request that he marry her, thinking it his duty, only to learn later that he had been brutally fooled. Indeed Arabella's girl-companions speak of his respect for duty when they advise her how to go about trapping him. Most of his sorrows might have been softened by his love for Sue Bridehead, but Hardy has tarnished it with so much sordidness that it does not seem to satisfy. Its partial ideality is ruined by the caprice with which Sue returns it, and that horrible anti-climax of his second marriage with Arabella. But the great tragedy of the story is obviously Jude's failure to attend the University of Christminster. This frustration is all the more tragic since we know of his ability to learn and his willingness to make extreme sacrifices for an education. The crushing of these hopes is one of the most pitiful things I have run across in any literature. Hardy is heartless in handling Jude. He not only refuses to

---

[1] *Jude*, p. 14
[2] *Ibid*, p. 73
[3] *Ibid*, p. 253

reward nobility of nature, but he even refuses to let it be its own reward. Jude's ideals are consistently uprooted until in that terrible last scene he gives expression to his resentment by wishing that he had never been born. At times there appears to be much of Job in him. Yes, he was, indeed a "predestinate Jude."[1] "He might battle with his evil stars," but he must finally submit to "the humours of things."[2]

There are so many references to Fate in *Jude* and *Tess* that it would be mere folly to list them here. In *Jude* the character who seems most conscious of a malignant Fate is Sue Bridehead. At first her attitude is one of hostility rather than resignation. Phillotson asks her, "who is (to blame) then? Am I?" She answers, "No—I don't know! The Universe, I suppose—things in general, because they are so horrid and cruel!"[3] Hardy perhaps considered it necessary to the tragedy of his plot that Jude should cling for a while to the Aeschylean belief in Fate, that he should have believed the early interventions of Fate in his endeavors as a kind of Divine Justice. He does not resign completely, for he still clings to free will. He goes so far as to believe that the Power above is interested in his welfare. "He took it as a good omen that numerous blocks of stone were lying about, which signified that the Cathedral was undergoing restoration or repairs to a considerable extent. It seemed to him, full of the superstitions of his beliefs, that this was an exercise of forethought on the part of a ruling Power, that he might find plenty to do in the art he practiced while waiting for a call to higher labours."[4] When Jude goes to see a hymn writer, in whom he is disappointed, he learns that he has missed a chance to see Sue. But, "at last his Chimerical expedition to Kennetbridge really did seem to have been another intervention of Providence to keep him away from temptation. But growing impatience of faith, which he had noticed in himself more than once of late, made him pass over in ridicule the idea that God sent people on fools' errands."[5] As Jude goes on, this doubt grows: "In the lonely room of his aunt's

---

[1] *Jude*, p. 45
[2] *Ibid*, p. 137
[3] *Jude*, p. 262
[4] *Ibid*, p. 154
[5] *Ibid*, p. 231

house Jude sat watching the cottage of the Widow Edlin as it disappeared behind the night shade. He knew that Sue was sitting within its walls equally lonely and disheartened; and again questioned his devotional motto that all was for the best."[1] What more complete disillusion could be cited than that final dying scene, as he, suffering the agony of thirst, utters with consummate contempt the lament of Job for his birth. "The President of the Immortals has ended his sport with Jude."

It is very clear that Jude is the victim of a determined state of things. His will is not free: character has no part in his destiny. Everything has been beyond his control. The exact nature of this system has been growing more definitely in Hardy's mind since his very early poems. There is a striking reference to it in a passage in *The Woodlanders:* "Hardly anything could be more isolated or more self-contained than the lives of these two walking here in the lonely antelucan hour, when gray shades, material and mental, are so very gray. And yet, looked at in a certain way, their lonely courses formed no detached design at all, but were part of the pattern in the great web of human doings then weaving in both hemispheres, from the White Sea to Cape Horn."[2] This comes close to the pictorial aspect of the Immanent Will of *The Dynasts*. There is a passage in Jude which anticipates significantly the philosophic conception which is soon to find expression in *The Dynasts*. Jude and Sue "would sit silent, more bodeful of the direct antagonism of things than of their insensate and stolid obstructiveness. Vague and quaint imaginings had haunted Sue in the days when her intellect scintillated like a star . . . that the First Cause worked automatically like a somnambulist, and not reflectively like a sage; that at the framing of the terrestial conditions there seemed never to have been contemplated such a development of emotional perceptiveness among the creatures subject to those conditions as that reached by thinking and educated humanity. But affliction makes opposing forces loom anthropomorphous."[3]

When Hardy completed *Jude,* he returned to poetry as a means

[1] *Jude*, p. 252
[2] *The Woodlanders*, p. 21
[3] *Jude*, p. 413, 407

of expressing with impunity a theory of determinism which he believed had grown too positive and bare to be expressed in prose. Owing to the fact that so few of his verses are dated, we cannot follow this development in a chronological manner from its origin in the "purblind Doomsters" of "Hap." Fate as mere Chance was bound to give way to Determinism in his verse as it had done in his prose, but the steps are not so clearly marked. Hardy's plan for *The Dynasts* was well in mind when he published his first volume of verse, "Wessex Poems" in 1898.[1] Part One of the Drama was published five years later. There are, however, a few short poems which seem to bridge the gap, and suggest the method by which he was to arrive at his final conception. This is referred to in "Nature's Questioning:"

> "Has some vast Imbecility,
>   Mighty to build and blend,
>   But impotent to tend,
> Framed us in jest, and left us not to hazardry?
>
> "Or come we of an Automaton
>   Unconscious of our pains?
>   Or are we live remains
> Of Godhead dying downward, brain and eye now gone?
>
> "Or is that some high Plan betides,
>   As yet not understood,
>   Of Evil stormed by Good,
> We the forlorn Hope over which Achievement strides?"[2]

We see him here groping for a definition. The same is true of "A Dream Question," in which he comes to a negative solution that the Almighty's ways are inscrutable, and that he often forgets man.[3] There is a vague idea of the Immanent Will in "Doom and She."[4] Blind nature asks Doom if all is well with her children, but he cannot tell for he knows not the meaning of Feeling or Right or Wrong. A better idea of this is found in "The Sleep Walker:"

---

[1] *Later Years*, p. 57
[2] *Collected Poems*, p. 59. From "Wessex Poems," 1898
[3] *Ibid*, p. 245. From "Times' Laughingstocks," 1909
[4] *Ibid*, p. 108. From "Poems of the Past and Present," 1901

> "When wilt thou wake, O Mother, wake and see—
> As one who, held in trance, has laboured long
> By vacant rote and prepossession strong—
> The coils that thou hast wrought unwittingly;
>
> .   .   .   .
>
> "Wilt thou destroy, in one wild shock of shame,
> Thy whole high heaving fermamental frame,
> Or patiently adjust, amend, and heal?"[1]

Here we see that Blind Nature's eyes may some day be opened, an idea that is more fully expressed in *The Dynasts*. Other poems which carry these same themes are: "The Subalterns;"[2] "Fragment;"[3] "The Aerolite;"[4] "Genitrix Laesa;"[5] and "The Bedridden Peasant."[6]

It is not the intention of this essay to treat the philosophical ramifications of Hardy's conception of the Immanent Will. This matter, especially as it is related to Schopenhauer, has been well defined by Ernest Brennecke in his *Thomas Hardy's Universe.* I shall be content to define the nature of its conception as it appears in *The Dynasts*, 1903-1908. It will be impossible to go into the intricate question of Hardy's elaborate spirit world as represented by his "phantoms" of his drama.

The Immanent Will, as has been said before, is Hardy's attempt to comprehend that force which rules the universe, and which has brought it to so much misery and woe. That this idea is connected with Schopenhauer and Hartmann I have shown. Hardy tells us that he used it in *The Dynasts* because, "some philosophy of life was necessary, and I went on using that which I had denoted in my previous volumes of verse (and to some extent prose) as being a generalized form of what the thinking world had gradually come to adopt, myself included."[7]

This is a manifestation of Determinism in a transcendental rather than mechanistic form. Philosophy defines it as Idealistic Monism. It refuses to accept a dualism of spirit and matter,

[1] *Collected Poems*, p. 110. From "Poems of the Past and Present," 1901.
[2] *Ibid*, p. 110. From "Poems of the Past and Present," 1901.
[3] *Ibid*, p. 482. From "Moments of Vision"
[4] *Ibid*, p. 736. From "Human Shows"
[5] *Ibid*, p. 737. From "Human Shows"
[6] *Ibid*, p. 113. From "Poems of the Past and Present," 1901
[7] *Later Years*, p. 124

as well as a materialistic concept. Spirit, for Hardy, is all; the Will is the dynamo of action. It is a genderless thing to which he refers with vagueness. The earth was created by it, and continues to be run by it. It unites all Nature and Time in somewhat the same way as does the Will of Schopenhauer.

In Hardy all actions originate in this Will. This is true of the most worthless insect just as it is of the Napoleonic debacle. All the destruction of joy and lives, all the coincidences, all sorrow and woes of the poems and novels spring from this all-powerful Force. Coincidences are by chance in that they have no purpose, not that they have no cause. The Will is within everything and above everything. Good and evil cannot conceive it, nor can joy and grief. It goes blindly on, weaving its web of fate, unconscious and unconcerned about its woof. It uses no check on error. This Will is without purpose, and Hardy holds that it rules a purposeless world as yet.

I have said "as yet" for it is basic in Hardy's theory that this "potter raptly planning" may be evolving toward consciousness. He thinks it possible that the day may come when this Force will realize the havoc it has wrought, and then perhaps set in motion some kind of machinery to bring the universe into harmony inherent in an immanent plan of Justice.

That consciousness of Fate which I have tried to trace through our author's actors assumes a definite form in *The Dynasts*, because by this period of his life, 1903-1908, his own conception of Fate has taken such a form. Only in Napoleon, however, is this idea embodied. This great ruler of Europe has an insight into the terrible truth and often cries out against it:

> "My star, my star is what's to blame—not I.
> It is unswervable."[1]

A more genuine poetic form is given his sense of determinism:

> "We are but thistle-globes on Heaven's high gales
> And whither blown, or when, or how, or why,
> Can choose us not at all!"[2]

---

[1] *The Dynasts*, p. 179
[2] *Ibid*, p. 204

While asleep he cries:

> "Why hold me my own master, if I be
> Ruled by the pitiless planet of Destiny?"[1]

Near the end of the drama he seems to be resigned to this Will:

> "As things are doomed to be they will be"[2]

At another time it is:

> "The Genius who outshapes my destinies . . . "[3]

At last he sees it correctly:

> "Yet, 'tis true, I have ever known
> That such a Will I passively obeyed!"[4]

Is it not possible that there is a Fate even above the Immanent Will which dooms it to weave on hopelessly without consciousness? Certainly Hardy did not think so.

Now comes one of the most inconsistent phases of Hardy's philosophy—a thing which would cause any philosopher to quibble. If this Immanent Will is consistently blind, why does it always blunder in such a manner as to be detrimental to man's happiness? Why does not Its blundering sometimes follow a kind of law of averages and turn to the good of man? And if It has not yet reached consciousness, how can mankind, who is but an humble part of It, have reached that condition? Can it be that we have not yet attained to that higher consciousness to which the transcendent Will had reached? This consciousness of the Will is one in which the meaninglessness of good and evil, joy and pain is manifest. If this be Hardy's reason, it is perhaps due to the fact that he is still a man of faith, who in the face of cruelty and injustice, refused to give up hope that a life devoted to goodness and truth is after all worthwhile, even though no reward may result. Does such a belief, if such be had, free him from the destructive charge of pessimism? Such a question is difficult to answer. Indeed, pessimism must be any contention that good never gets its reward in life, and that there can be no

---

[1] *The Dynasts*, p. 468
[2] *Ibid*, p. 401
[3] *Ibid*, p. 363
[4] *Ibid*, p. 519

justice.   But the mere fact that Hardy has faith in the desirability of goodness and truth lends his works an interest for us which otherwise they could not possess.

That Hardy's conception of Fate is an aid to his art as forming a poetic vision I have already stated.   By its use he obtained an epic view of things, horrible in its comprehensiveness, moving in its grandeur.   For the choir of spirits who reflect the Will's decrees comment in poetry that is significant and beautiful. When we see the workings of this Immanent Will in the following passage, we get a picture that is awe inspiring to the point of actual sublimity: "At once as earlier, a preternatural clearness possesses the atmosphere of the battle-field, in which the scene becomes anatomized and the living masses of humanity transparent. The controlling Immanent Will appears therein, as a brain-like network of currents and ejections, twitching, interpenetrating, entangling, and thrusting hither and thither the human forms."[1]

In the chapters which follow I shall demonstrate how Hardy has used this favorite motif in five manifestations, which constitute his artistic anatomy of Fate.

---

[1] *The Dynasts*, p. 118

CHAPTER III

CHANCE AND COINCIDENCE

Fate appears in Hardy's works as an artistic motif in a great variety of forms which I shall consider as five: Chance and Coincidence, Nature, Time, Woman, and Convention. I think this an original method of approaching the subject; yet this classification is no arbitrary device of mine. All of these terms are found often in his prose and verse, and while Hardy never classified them in this manner, I have no doubt that he considered them as important motifs of Fate. It is not to be thought that any of these is Fate itself; however, they are all manifestations of the Immanent Will. Of these five forms, I think Nature comes nearest being analogous to this Immanent Will.

It is seen that all of these forms of Destiny are external to Man—and Woman also—for we shall see how Hardy views his world through Man's eye, while in Woman there exists a nature as direful as those of Coincidence and Time in bringing Man to destruction. Woman is not only a victim of Fate, but she is even Fate's instrument in a way very different from that in which all human beings are parts of the Immanent Will. Hardy's characters run true to types notwithstanding apparent individuality. This is true to the extent that it is possible to trace the development of types through his works, as I shall do later. In these types we shall see that his women in general possess inherent characteristics of sex put there by Destiny to entrap men. Man is powerless to deliver himself, but Woman is irresponsible.

I have stated that to Hardy, Fate is a force external to Man. In other words, Character is not Fate. Man is often destroyed by instinct, of course, but Hardy hardly ever sees it this way. Human beings are not brought to grief because of instinctive love of goodness, but they are dragged down by the forces outside them which defeat it. Man is not ruined by his sexual instinct, but by the irresponsible nature of Woman. Jude is not brought to disillusion by ambition, but by a cruel and heartless convention which denies this ambition. After all, Man's instinctive longing for joy is not to blame, but Fate which uses its forces to defeat this desire. Man's point of view appeals to Hardy, and he works on that basis from the beginning.

These instruments themselves are not to be considered as necessarily malicious, though they do manifest a malignant Power. Hardy fails to make this very clear, but concerning the part that Woman, whom he motivates more clearly than others, plays, it appears that, though they submit to being used in this way, they do not contribute any individual hostility to that of the Will of which they form a part. Still the antithesis of this statement is suggested by certain allusions to the cruelty of Time and Chance, especially in his verse. Perhaps the man desired to leave the entire matter of individuality vague in his determined system. It is safe to say, however, that he allowed each of his actors a kind of individuality—otherwise there could be no tragic action. He believed each of the infinite number of ends or bits of the Immanent Will to be in a very real respect an individual, and just as each spirit in the choir of *The Dynasts* is individualized, so is each man on his earth.

First consideration in this analysis is due, I think, to Chance and Coincidence, because it was the first tool of Fate to mature in Hardy's mind, and is most often noticed in his early works. We see it fully developed in *Desperate Remedies*, perhaps because it is a device often used by beginners. Hardy, however, was to give its employment a peculiar significance.

I have decided to substitute the term "Coincidence" or "Fateful Incident" in order to describe this motif, because we usually think of the word "Chance" as indicating mere accident, a force which would render a determined system impossible and void. The former terms seem more serviceable since they carry no element of "mere Chance" or "wanton Chance." We have observed how Hardy's philosophy has been a development from a conception of the Universe as chaotic, ruled by Chance to a world ruled by determinism. Noticeable or surprising concurrences of events, which we here call "Coincidences", have been characteristic of Hardy's plots in all periods of his career, and they have usually proved links in a concatenation of incidents tending toward evil; but in his first books they are interpreted as having no determined causes. In later ones they are parts of a determined system and consequently only seem to be accidents.

Hardy is so persistent in his use of Coincidence that his plots almost break under the strain, but this device is as closely allied to artistic effectiveness as it is to his philosophy. Our chief interest here is the effect of Coincidence on the reality of his work. Was Hardy guilty of sacrificing his art in the interest of truth to his way of interpreting life? Like so many questions of its kind, it is not easy to answer.

As we search his plots for Coincidence, we are impressed by the fact that he uses this force not so much to interpret the unrelenting trend of his action, but to further it. In novels of his late life, coincidences are allied with a unity of purpose which persuades us that they are not only parts of a determined system, but parts of a system determined for evil. Event links up with event in a preconceived plan for evil. Compare such a conception with that of Chance in our cheap modern stories, in which one final coincidence for good is thrown in after a series of evil ones, the final one cancelling the evil effects of the others. But in Hardy, who rarely yielded to the clamor for happy endings, there can be no such end; the last coincidence is as bad, or worse, than its predecessors. Even though this malignant Coincidence has its origin in the Will, it strains plausibility just as much as that of the cheaper story with the happy coincidence at the conclusion. Even though the trend of the plot is furthered by its use, it is a kind of trick, an easy way out. Some writers, who have not been able to get themselves out of their own created situation, have used this method as one of escape. It appears that this idea may have been in Hardy's mind, when upon the first publication of *The Mayor of Casterbridge*, he wrote in his journal: "I fear it will not be so good as I meant, but after all, it is not improbabilities of incident but improbabilities of character that matter."[1]

I have but little belief that such an accusation is just, because he possessed a peculiar outlook which seems basic to a compre-

---

[1]*Early Life*, p. 231

hension of the Coincidence motif. That is to say, he had an absorbing interest in incidents or circumstance, which is connected with his persistent concern with external realities.[1] He always thought of life in terms of action; likewise, he thought of action in terms of incident. A great deal lies behind that statement in his journal which says: "In a work of art it is the accident which *Charms*, not the intention; *that* we only like and admire."[2] Coincidence was interesting to Hardy for other than fatal purposes. He was impressed by its bare irony. "Satires of Circumstance" do not always display a malignant nature, but they do always suggest irony. His chief concern, however, seems to be that a lifetime of joy should depend on a minor circumstance. Perhaps the best instance of this is the poem, "The Gap in the White", in which the heroine breaks her front tooth, ruins her love, and loses her life.[3]

Coincidence is given a negative as well as a positive aspect. We often realize that Coincidences could have taken place but did not. Hardy would say, "because they never do"; meetings which might have saved many lives are allowed to miss by a few moments. I am not referring to such instances as Fanny Robin's failure to meet Troy at the church; that is a variation of positive Coincidence. I refer to those which no force, human or transcendent, planned for, yet which we feel might have occurred if frustration and evil had not appeared. The mere suggesting of these negative types of his motif seems to please Hardy. A good example of this use is found in the first pages of *Tess*. Angel Clare, with his two brothers, passes through Tess's village and sees her and her companions dancing on the green. He looks on for a while and then chooses a partner. He "took almost the first that came to hand", but he didn't take Tess.[4] After dancing a short time he left, not having noticed her at all. There can be but one reason why Hardy introduces this episode: to sting us with the thought that if Clare had selected Tess for his dancing mate, both of them would have escaped their tragic end. Its

---

[1] *Ante*, pp. 36
[2] *Early Life*, p. 251
[3] *Winter Words*, p. 182
[4] *Tess*, p. 16

prime illustration, however, is found in *Jude*. Hardy says that "somebody might have come along that way who would have asked him his trouble; but nobody did come, because nobody does."[1] And Hardy should have added, to be consistent: But if evil were to be accomplished, depend upon it, somebody would.

There are various forms of Fateful Incident in Hardy's works. Some of these are mere annoying tricks, often used by mediocre writers. The overheard conversation is one which is both weak and overworked. There are three instances of it in *Desperate Remedies*. Coming as they do at a crucial part of the plot, they exercise a most profound effect on the complications of the novel. The device is, indeed, strained when Manston overhears the villager's account at the inn relative to his part in his wife's death. This information leads him to employ Anne to appear as his wife. This relation with Anne eventually proves his downfall. In *A Pair of Blue Eyes* when Stephen has returned from India, he overhears a conversation of love between Knight and Elfride, and his relation to the girl is irreparably changed. The purposely farcical event in *The Hand of Ethelberta*, in which Ladywell and Neigh overhear Ethelberta flirting with Montclere, is less open to criticism. Somerset's happiness is delayed by Dare's overhearing a conversation between Somerset and Paula in *A Laodicean*. But the most tragic of all is the incident near the beginning of *The Woodlanders*, when Marty South, devoted to Giles, hears the conversation about the union of Grace and Giles, and as a result she becomes resigned, eats her honest heart out with grief, and courts neglect.

La Feste, the hero of "Alicia's Diary", (1887) hears two sisters who are in love with him talking. While he really is in love with the older one, he is bound by a former promise, to marry the younger sister. From their conversation he learns that the older one loves him too; therefore, he determines to marry her.[2]

The heroine in "Lady Penelope" is married successively to three suitors of her youth and the villagers have it that she killed the second in order to fulfill her vow to wed all three. "The Mansion that she had occupied had been left to her for so long

---

[1] *Jude*, p. 29
[2] *A Changed Man*

a time as she should choose to reside in it, and having a regard for the spot, she had coaxed Sir William to remain there. But in the end it was unfortunate; for one day, when in the full tide of his happiness, he was walking among the willows near the gardens, where he overheard a conversation between some basket-makers who were cutting the osiers for their use. In this fatal dialogue the suspicion of the neighboring townsfolk was revealed to him for the first time."[1] This revelation prompts him to leave her, after which she soon dies. When it is too late, he learns from her physician that Penelope did not murder her second husband.

Such methods are not confined to Hardy's minor works; his best books contain them. Had Tess failed to hear Clare's brothers talking about her when she went to see his parents at Emminster, she might have escaped her final tragedy and been reunited with her husband.[2] Cowed by their bitterness toward her, she went back to the farm, not knowing that the father of these boys was a kind old man who would have aided her in her sorrow.

In the persistent use of this overheard conversation there is something not very pleasing, even though it be an element in a system of Coincidence. Another trite form of this motif is an undelivered letter or a marriage license issued for the wrong place or date. The manifestation of Fate through a technicality of Law, seen in the latter becomes irritating because we know this hitch occurs mush less frequently in life than that of the un-delivered letter or the overheard conversation. Recalling the peculiar demands of Hardy's system, the criterion by which these coincidences must be judged is that of reality and credibility.

I shall now attempt to show how Hardy's system progressed from Chance to Determinism and how it is suggested in his artistic use of Coincidence. In his early works that concatenation of numerous circumstances toward one end is absent. There is not that same tight linking of incidents toward doom which appears later. Here joy or grief oftener hinges on a single incident, or even on a few circumstances set opposite others. This is

---

[1] *A Group of Noble Dames*, p. 185
[2] *Tess*, p. 343-44

involved in a happy ending, in which good circumstances of the present overpower evil ones of the past. Apropos of this I do not believe Hardy was altogether hostile to "happy endings", but probably looked upon them as a kind of negation. He would certainly have admitted that the *Mayor of Casterbridge*, *Tess* and *Jude* have unhappy endings. On the other hand, he would have contended that *Far from the Madding Crowd*, *The Hand of Ethelberta*, *Two on a Tower*, and *The Woodlanders* have happy endings,—as happy, that is, as we may expect them to be in life. But his conviction must have suffered when he penned the conclusions of *Desperate Remedies*, *Under the Greenwood Tree*, and *A Laodicean*. The man's mind simply did not lend itself to happy endings, and to make his actors merely not unhappy was about as far as he could go.

When the student begins to trace tendencies in Hardy, he is thankful for that first novel, *Desperate Remedies*. Immature as it obviously is, it shows a, less veiled use of some essentials of his art, which were to be refined and subdued in subsequent books. A glance at this novel enables us to understand the development of Coincidence much more readily than does the romance, *Under the Greenwood Tree*. Coincidence is the very core of its plot. There are so many of them that I can consider only the most essential of them here. Is it not extraordinary that the old gate-keeper should tell Owen of the old woman whom he aided as long ago as 1834? Then, too, Cytherea's career is influenced by Manston's failure to meet his wife at the railway station. She is also upset by the accident in which Owen injures his foot, for incapacitated as he is, he is led to advise Cytherea to accept Manston's proposal of marriage as a sign of appreciation for the latter's help to him while he was injured. Then, to make Coincidence more ironical still, Owen's foot heals just before the marriage day arrives. Now and then, Chance appears on the side of conventional morality. The porter tells Owen and Edward of Eunice's escape from the fire on the very day that Manston and Cytherea marry and go to France. Propriety dictates that they must be overtaken. Here are four incidents: two are for good, two for evil. Many coincidences in the book have no unrelenting purpose, but serve to carry the action by surprises.

Hardy does, in one case, give a suggestion of the method as it occurs in later books. Cytherea and Owen are talking:

"Do you believe in such odd coincidences?"

"How do you mean, believe in them? They occur sometimes. Yes, one will occur often enough—that is, two disconnected events will fall strangely together by chance, and people scarcely notice the fact beyond saying, 'Oddly enough it happened that so and so were the same', and so on. But when three such events coincide, withstanding any apparent reason for the coincidence, it seems as if there must be invisible means at work."[1]

In that excellent story, *A Pair of Blue Eyes*, the idea is made more definite. Here accidents prevail as mere happenings. There is often irony bound up in Coincidence, as where Knight and Smith, teacher and pupil, become rivals. Another of the same kind is having Mrs. Jethway placed on the tomb of her dead son. She had been the avenging instrument of her son, who had been jilted by Elfride. There is symbolism in the sociable chess game in which Stephen is beaten by Elfride, but she in turn always loses to Knight. The fall of the tower just as Elfride has finished saying, "Thou hast been my hope and a strong tower for me against the enemy" is a definite instance of it.[2] When this tower falls, it falls on Mrs. Jethway who was walking under it. But she is not crushed until she has mailed to Knight a letter which is destined to wreck Elfride. So many coincidences, jammed one against the other in this way, strain our patience at times. Mrs. Jethway, whose chief aim in life is to injure Elfride, is often assisted by Chance. When Elfride and Stephen lose their resolve and fail to be married, she happens to be at the station when they alight from the train. Again she haunts Elfride when she threatens on the boat to reveal the girl's past. This "past" which the woman threatens to reveal is the juvenile affair of Elfride and Mrs. Jethway's son, a good example of frustration, above mentioned in which an unwise choice made in youth serves to wreck future happiness.

A good example of Coincidence is the finding of the lost earring in the rock crevice just at the most crucial moment with Knight. She had lost the piece of jewelry at the moment when Stephen

[1] *Desperate Remedies*, p. 168
[2] *A Pair of Blue Eyes*, p. 356

had kissed her. To increase the irony of this situation, we learn that for only a short period each day, when the sun shines in the crevice, could this article be observed. The crowning coincidence of the book lies in the fact that Knight and Stephen take the same train by accident in order to claim Elfride, who, having died in London, without their knowledge, is being borne a corpse on the same train with them. An excellent book though it is, it resolves structurally into a series of accidental happenings piled up to one crowning coincidence. That there may be another hand in these things seems evident to Elfride when we are told that "there seemed to be a special facility offered by a power external to herself in the circumstance that Mr. Swancourt had proposed to leave home the night previous to her wished-for day."[1] There was indeed, for both father and daughter had gone off with a secret intention of marrying.

When we study *Far From The Madding Crowd*, we find coincidence a far less essential motif in that it is not used often to move the plot. Of course, there are a few cases of it, such as the one in which Fanny Robin goes to the wrong church to be married to Troy. In this same connection is another chance which starts a chain of events which lead to sorrow. Joseph Poorgrass, driving the dead-wagon in which Fanny Robin's body is reposing, stops at an inn for refreshments. This causes the delay of the burial, and the body has to be carried to Bathsheba's house, where she, in order to allay her suspicions, opens the casket and finds Troy's baby lying in Fanny's arms. Sergeant Troy's affection for Fanny is somewhat revived by this horrible episode, and as a consequence, happiness is destroyed for him and Bathsheba. Fate has a tantalizing trick of throwing Troy in Boldwood's path at the most crucial moments. Bathsheba meets Troy on the very night that she refuses to respond to Boldwood's offer of wedlock. This same Troy, long after he is thought to be drowned, turns up as an actor in a circus, and wrecks the farmer's hopes when success in winning Bathsheba seems to be within his grasp. Frustration is in these cases brought about by Chance.

---

[1]*A Pair of Blue Eyes*, p. 110

One Coincidence in the early pages of *The Hand of Ethelberta* accounts for the heroine's entire career. The girl had written some verses which offended her guardian, Lady Petherwin, and for this act the Lady cuts her out of her will. Lady Petherwin repents this hasty act, but dies before it can be corrected. Left without money, Ethelberta is forced to a frugal and tricky mode of living. Sol and Chickerel arrive at Knocksea just a moment too late to prevent the marriage of the girl and Mountclere. Chance decreed that the wedding should go on.

Chance and Coincidence play a subordinate part in *The Return of the Native*. Determinism has taken its place. There is only one essential instance of Chance in the story, and that one is responsible for the final catastrophe of the action. It is the well known scene in which Eustacia neglects to go to the door when Mrs. Yeobright knocks at Clym's house, where she has come for reconciliation with her son. The poor woman, broken in heart, goes away, for she thinks her son, who is in reality sound asleep and has not heard her, has purposely turned her away. Clym soon awakes and goes off toward his mother's house for the same purpose for which she had so recently come to his—to be reconciled to her. On his way over the Heath he discovers his mother in a dying condition, and in spite of all he can do to save her, she succumbs during the night. This event proves Eustacia's undoing later on. There are other appearances of Chance in the two wierd dice games between Wildeve and the Reddleman, in which the latter plays for and wins Mrs. Yeobright's money with a consistency unknown to the cleverest dice thrower.

Chance brings on both good and evil in *A Laodicean*. Somerset goes to meet Paula, but instead he meets the rascal Dare, who has lost his money at cards at Monte Carlo. Here starts a series of incidents which bring woe to Somerset. But this event has a happy issue, for on the very day that Paula is to marry De Stancy, Charlotte learns that Dare has maliciously libelled Somerset's character. On this event hangs the happy ending of the novel. Earlier in the novel Hardy expresses disgust at the cruelty of Chance: "It was one of those gratuitous encounters which only happen to discarded lovers who have shown commendable stoicism under disappointment, as if on purpose to reopen and aggravate their wounds."[1]

In *Two on a Tower* there is a peculiar interest in the motif of Coincidence. This is probably due to the fact that the improbability of Chance is less culpable in lighter works. It occurs here near the end of the plot, and only by violent twisting does it bring temporary joy to Swithin and Viviette. She has secretly married Swithin, sure that she is a widow; therefore, when the Bishop of Manchester proposes, she promptly refuses him. Immediately, word comes that her first husband had not died until after her secret marriage with Swithin. She realizes that she and her lover must be married again, when she is led to refrain by finding papers stating that he is to receive a large sum of money if he does not marry before he is twenty-five years old. To remove all chance of marriage, she, in a spirit of sacrifice, ships the young man off to South Africa to complete his studies in astronomy. He has barely lost sight of land, when she discovers that she is to become a mother. She tries to locate him, but he has gone. By Chance, the Bishop proposes again and is promptly accepted. Soon after the birth of a son, the Bishop conveniently dies, and by Chance Swithin returns to marry Viviette. He is shocked at her haggard appearance, appears unduly cool toward her, proposes reluctantly, she accepts him and dies in his arms.

Hardy handles these remarkable incidents with consummate skill, and it is possible that because of the prevalence of this motif, critics have failed to value it properly. A symbolical use of Chance occurs in the coming of the storm which tears the top off Swithin's tower to stultify the doubt of its power which he had just expressed.[2] The same motif occurs when Swithin puts on Sir Blount's suit of clothes unwittingly.[3] That accident in which Viviette's brother's horse lash strikes her in the dark is just beyond our conception of Chance.[4] In this romance, Hardy is making too much use of Chance.

Yet this was the swan-song of that phase of his motif. In the

---

[1] *A Laodicean*, p. 368
[1] *Two on a Tower*, p. 119
[3] *Ibid*, p. 162
[4] *Ibid*, p. 144

last four great novels, inevitable determinism replaces mere Chance as a controlling force. Coincidence still plays a part, but only as an instrument of Determinism. For the Mayor of Casterbridge is doomed from the moment he drinks at the furmity tent at Weydon Priors. The instruments of Fate set in action their machinery to punish him. There is no let up or mercy in the action; the trend is mercilessly clear. Such fateful incidents as the appearance of the long lost Newsom at the inopportune time, and Henchard's being destined to prosecute the old furmity woman are natural parts of a relentless plan. Lucetta and not the Mayor is involved in the one outstanding accident of the story, where Lucetta's love letters are given for delivery to the old gossip Jopp who reads them in the tavern. This act results in the frightful "skimmity" ride and the resultant death of Lucetta.

Fateful Incident, without the provocation which urged it on to destroy Henchard, moved likewise against Giles in *The Woodlanders*. He is completely borne down by it from that day on which he chanced to meet Felice on the highway and offended her to the point where she declined to grant him longer leases on her property which he loses as the result of a group of coincidences.

In *Tess* this is more certainly true. There are many Fateful Incidents—Durbeyfield's learning of his lineage, the killing of the old horse, the child resulting from the seduction, the series of events which frustrates Tess's attempt to confess to Angel, culminating in the letter under the carpet, the death of her father, which plays her into Alec's hands again, and the return of Angel just too late—but all are parts of a determined series. Nothing here is done by Chance. Tess, like Romeo and Juliet, is doomed from the beginning. Hardy says of her: "Nature does not often say, 'See' to a poor creature at a time when seeing can lead to happy doing; or reply, 'Here' to a body's cry of 'Where?' till the hide-and-seek has become an irksome, outworn game. We may wonder whether at the acme and summit of human progress these anachronisms will become corrected by a finer intuition, a closer interaction of the social machinery than that which now jolts us round and long; but such completeness is not to be prophesied, or even conceived as possible. Enough that in the present case, as in millions, it was not the two halves of a perfect whole that confronted each other at the perfect moment; part and counterpart wandered independently about the earth in the stupidest manner possible till the late time came. Out of which maladroit delay sprang anxieties, disappointments, shocks, catastrophes, and passing strange destinies."[1]

Very much the same is true of *Jude*. The appearance of Chance here as a manifestation of Fate is infrequent. Examples are Jude's first meeting with Arabella, and the other meeting with her when she is a bar maid in the tavern. Both of these coincidences hurry Jude on to ruin.

It is difficult to point to Coincidence and Chance in the poems because they are so short that it becomes impossible to gather many incidents. Everything usually depends upon just one circumstance. In "The Newcomer's Wife",[2] an overheard conversation informs the husband that his wife is more experienced in love affairs than she should be, whereupon he drowns himself. "The Wedding Morn" is similar; in it, the wife overhears the husband declare his preference for another girl.[3]

"A Sunday Morning Tragedy" is one of the most pathetic of this kind.[4] In "A Conversation at Dawn" lives are wrecked because of unrealized passions.[5] "The Whaler's Wife" is an example of tragic misunderstanding. The whaler, hearing that his wife had been visited by a man in his absence, believes her untrue and deserts her. The visitor was actually her father, but no one knew it.[6] "The Torn Letter", in which the reader carelessly destroys the letter and then realizes he has made a mistake, is a varied conception of frustration.[7] As long as he lives he pines for the unknown writer. Chance and Coincidence often appear in lighter forms. This is true in "The Contretemps" where a wife who is eloping from her husband runs into the arms of a poet instead of her lover. They become resigned to circum-

[1]*Tess*, p. 44
[2]*Collected Poems*, p. 344, from "Satires of Circumstance"
[3]*Collected Poems*, p. 572, from "Late Lyrics and Earlier"
[4]*Collected Poems*, p. 188, from "Time's Laughingstocks"
[5]*Collected Poems*, p. 344, from "Satires of Circumstance"
[6]*Winter Words*, p. 45
[7]*Collected Poems*, p. 294, from "Satires of Circumstance"

stances and marry.[1]   The highly improbable "Kiss in the Dark"
is another example of this motif.

Fateful Incident is the most obvious of the motifs of Fate in
Hardy's works.   In his early period it outweighs all the other
motifs in importance with disastrous effects to the credibility
and reality of his plots.   In later years it was tamed to place
as one of the manifestations of a determined system.   It ceased
to be wanton Chance and took its position as an instrument of
hostile Fate.   Though it thus acquired purpose of a malignant
sort, it could never lose wholly that element of the improbable
which it must ever hold for those who do not interpret the action
of life, with Hardy, in terms of Incident.

---

[1]*Collected Poems*, p. 551, from "Late Lyrics and Earlier"

CHAPTER IV

TIME

Hardy has shown very clearly in his works that he considers Time a principal manifestation of Fate.   In the title of his third volume of poems, *Satires of Circumstance*, he used Fateful Incident as a motif; and in the second, *Time's Laughingstocks*, the Time motif is embodied.   In his early poems these two motifs were employed frequently, and even in his later system they were not forgotten.   Time appears prominently in *The Dynasts*, though somewhat altered, as the Spirit of the Years.   Here, much of its sinister nature has been lost, however.   It explains its characteristics:

> " . . . ask the Immanent!
> I am but an accessory of Its works
> Whom the Ages render conscious, and at most
> Figure as bounden witness of Its laws.'"[1]

The motif of Time has two chief uses in Hardy: the tremendous importance of the moment, and the disillusionment and change which come with the years.   The first emphasizes how much may depend on only a few seconds; the other how little really matters in a thousand years or more.   The importance of the moment has much in common with the Fateful Incident.   It emphasizes the essential importance of little things, and no doubt originated in Hardy's interpretation of life in terms of the external —a feature of his philosophy that we have noticed before.   For him Time was a great series of moments, just as life was action, and action was incident,—each one perhaps laden with sorrow and pain for someone.   The poem, "That Moment" very significantly states the case:

> "The tragedy of that moment
> Was deeper than the sea,
> When I came in that moment
> And heard you speak to me!

---

[1] *The Dynasts*, p. 15

"What I could not help seeing
Covered life as a blot;
Yes, that which I was seeing
And knew that you were not."[1]

It is often difficult, nevertheless, to distinguish this from
incident, so closely are the two allied. Fate, in the short story,
"The Hardcombes", conspires through incident to drown the
two adventurous lovers in each other's arms in order that two
less brave ones might marry. As an instance of Time let us
consider the case of Jocelyn, who in *The Well Beloved*, cannot
obtain a legal permit to wed Marcia at the very time when she
was willing to be his wife. When he does find it possible to secure
the license, she has changed her mind and refuses him. This
is frustration, perhaps of a fortunate kind, by Time. Often we
find the two motifs of incident and Time bound into one. In
The Woodlanders, old Mr. South dies as the tree crashes to the
ground just before Winterbourne was able to renew his lease on
the property, which at the death of South, leaves the boy without
a home in which to live. Since there are so many of these com-
pound examples, I shall not attempt to enumerate them.

Hardy uses the second of these motifs, change and disillusionment which the years bring, much more definitely than the first
one, the importance of the moment. Time, the bringer of all
things, is usually the bringer of regret, decay and death. It is
a symbol of tragedy wrought by the carrying out of the eternal
edict that "Even this must pass away". It is indicated by the
Spirit of the Years, who says:

Men pass to dark corruption, at the best,
Ere I can count five score.'[2]

The unrelenting attack of Time on our illusions is the most
important of these subdivisions of the idea. The greatest of
these, we are to believe, is happiness. In Hardy this illusion is
sufficiently real while it endures, but it cannot endure long, and
therein lies the tragedy. The joys of life appear to him as transitory; their place is taken by sorrow and grief in various forms.
These moments of joy are turned to bitterness by Time.

[1]*Collected Poems*, 786, from "Human Shows; Far Phantasies".
[2]*The Dynasts*, p. 253

Time is personified all through Hardy's writings. Especially does it so appear in his verse as a Disillusioner, where, as we should expect, the motifs are most definitely expressed. It appears as "dicing time" in "Hap", one of the earliest of his poems. Here it is one of the "purblind Doomsters."[1] It also occurs in "My Cicely" in an interesting form:

> "Too mocking to Love's re-expression
> Was Time's repartee!"[2]

In "Lines" an orphaned child is addressed:

> "O wondering child, unwitting Time's design,
> Why should Man add to Nature's quandary
> And worsen ill by thus immuring thee?"[3]

He speaks of "Time's transforming chisel", "The Revisitation."[4] In "The Flirt's Tragedy" "Time unveils sorrows and secrets."[5] In "Panthera" it is the "cynic Time."[6]

We are plunged into the "den of Time" in "A Plaint to Man" (1909)[7]. The inevitability of "Time's stayless stealthy swing" is seen in "God's Funeral."[8] "Time's unflinching rigour" is pictured in "At Castle Boterel" (1913).[9] It is "Time's derision" in "After a Journey;"[10] "Time laughed awry" in "At the Piano;"[11] and, "An unconscienced trick of Time" is shown us in "The Pedestrian."[12] Time is personified less frequently in the novels, yet there are many cases even there. In *Desperate Remedies* we have "Time the Improver."[13] It is "Time the Cynic" in *A Pair of Blue Eyes*.[14] "Time had at last brought about his revenges" on Viviette in *Two on a Tower*.[15]

[1]*Collected Poems*, p. 7, from "Wessex Poems."
[2]*Collected Poems*, p. 47, from "Wessex Poems."
[3]*Collected Poems*, p. 71, from "Wessex Poems."
[4]*Collected Poems*, p. 177, from "Time's Laughingstocks."
[5]*Collected Poems*, p. 198 from "Time's Laughingstocks."
[6]*Collected Poems*, p. 262, from "Time's Laughingstocks."
[7]*Collected Poems*, p. 306, from "Time's Laughingstocks."
[8]*Collected Poems*, p. 308, from "Time's Laughingstocks."
[9]*Collected Poems*, p. 331, from "Time's Laughingstocks."
[10]*Collected Poems*, p. 328, from "Time's Laughingstocks."
[11]*Collected Poems*, p. 497, from "Satires of Circumstance."
[12]*Collected Poems*, p. 473, from "Satires of Circumstance."
[13]*Desperate Remedies*, p. 126.
[14]*A Pair of Blue Eyes*, p. 289.
[15]*Two on a Tower*, p. 311.

"Time the Magician" we see in *The Mayor of Casterbridge*.[1] Marty South's beautiful hair is "Time's one gift to the particular victim of his now before us", of *The Woodlanders*.[2] In *Tess*, as it was first published in America, the "President of the Immortals," in the end of the story, was spoken to as "Time the Archsatirist." The supreme example of personification is the grotesque fact that Arabella's child is nicknamed "Father Time." The first sketches for *The Well Beloved*, we must recall, were called *Time Against Two*.[3]

These examples taken from Hardy's works of all the periods are sufficient to prove that the author thought of this motif as a definite theme. Of the five motifs under discussion, Time was one of the earliest to interest him and it went through very few changes after his first use of it.

Time's victory over illusions expresses again what we have several times mentioned of Hardy: his skepticism of self-stimulated and self-contained happiness. He contends unflinchingly for the essential force of external influences, and severe critics of the man might with some reason declare that for Hardy happiness is a rather superficial thing. On the score of joy, none of his characters is self-sufficient—which may be no more than a faithful reading of life.

In Time's victory over illusions, love is usually the thing concerned, for it appears that Hardy considered it to be a source of most of the important conditions of life. The existence of Time makes disillusion inevitable. Happiness depends upon temporary things—things which are subject to Time. Life and Time are rivals in a great race, but a losing one for Life. To die is to be "Time-outrun."[4] One of the chief joys of life is love, and in order to crush the illusion of happiness, Hardy strikes at its chief instrument.

This idea is found in one of the earliest poems, "The Dawn After the Dance" (1869). Here love is destroyed because of its

[1] *The Mayor of Casterbridge*, p. 37.
[2] *The Woodlanders*, p. 9.
[3] *Early Life*, p. 215.
[4] *Winter Words*, "After the Death of a Friend." p. 59.

own ardor: "Yet we dreamt us but beginning a sweet sempiternal spinning, of a cord we have spun to breaking—too intemperately, too well."[1]

> "That which makes man's love the lighter and the
> woman's burn no brighter
> Came to pass with us inevitably while slipped the
> shortening year."[2]

In the little poem, "Postponement" (1866), even the little snow-bound bird laments the fact that Time annihilates love.[3]

In "Her Initials" (1869), is a very definite statement of the early conception of Time:

> "Upon a poet's page I wrote
> Of old two letters of her name;
> Part seemed she of the effulgent thought
> Whence that high singer's rapture came,
> —When now I turn the leaf the same
> Immortal light illumes the lay,
> But from the letters of her name
> The radiance has waned away."[4]

In the triolet "At a Hasty Wedding" is a very delicate statement of this idea:

> "If hours be years the twain are blest,
> For now they solace swift desire
> By bonds of every bond the best,
> If hours be years. The twain are blest . . ." [5]

Hardy says later on that "Time cures hearts of tenderness."[6] But again he indicates that man is the chief offender:

> "Time, that dooms man's love to die
> Preserves a maid's alive."[7]

---

[1]*Collected Poems*, p. 214, from "Time's Laughingstocks."
[2]*Collected Poems*, p. 214, from "Time's Laughingstocks."
[3]*Collected Poems*, p. 8, from "Wessex Poems."
[4]*Collected Poems*, p. 10, from "Wessex Poems."
[5]*Collected Poems*, p. 130, from "Past and Present."
[6]*Collected Poems*, p. 301 "Wessex Heights", from "Satires of Circumstance."
[7]*Collected Poems*, p. 225, "The Inquiry", from "Time's Laughingstocks."

Just one year prior to Hardy's death, he wrote this melancholy idea into that forlorn poem, "Seeing the Moon Rise:"

> "We used to go to Froom-hill Barrow
> To see the round moon rise
> Into the heath-rimmed skies,
> Trudging thither by plough and harrow
> Up the pathway, steep and narrow,
> Singing a song.
> Now we do not go there. Why?
> Zest burns not so high."[1]

The decay of beauty, often allied to disillusionment in love, is often the object of Time's attacks.   In an early poem, "She to Him" (1866), Hardy shows the beloved entreating her lover:

> "When you see me in the toils of Time,
> My lauded beauties carried off from me,
> My eyes no longer stars as in their prime,
> My name forgot of Maiden Fair and Free;—
> Remembering mine the loss is, not the blame,
> That Sportsman Time but rears his brood to kill,
> Knowing me in my soul the very same—
> One who would die to spare you touch of ill!
> Will you not grant to old affection's claim
> The hand of friendship down Life's sunless hill?"[2]

On occasion this motif of Time is heartlessly cruel: it shrivels the skin, but the heart burns on in its youthful passion:

> "But Time, to make me grieve,
> Part steals, lets part abide;
> And shakes this fragile frame at eve
> With throbbings of noontide."[3]

The opposite of this is expressed in "The Dream Follower", in which a lover's dream flies to his old love:

> "And I saw but a thing of flesh and bone
> Speeding on to its cleft in the clay;
> And my dream was scared, and expired on a moan,
> And I whitely hastened away."[4]

---

[1] *Winter Words*, p. 111
[2] *Collected Poems*, p. 11, from "Wessex Poems."
[3] *Collected Poems*, p. 72, "I Look into my Glass," from "Wessex Poems."
[4] *Collected Poems*, p. 130, from "Wessex Poems"

The lover, in "In The Night She Came" assures his beloved that "Time's mere assault would work no change" in his love. But that very night she appeared before him "toothless, and wan, and old, with leaden concaves around her eyes, and wrinkles manifold." Time had done its worst; for, the next time they saw each other they seemed "divided like a shade."[1] "Time, 'in his own grey style', taught Farfrae how to estimate his experience of Lucetta—all that it was, and all that it was not."

This assault of Time on Love is more definitely commented on in *Tess*: "He (Angel) knew, and she knew, that, though the fascination which each had exercised over the other—on her part independently of accomplishments—would probably, in the first days of their separation be more potent than ever, time must attenuate that effect . . . when two people are once parted . . . new growths insensibly bud upwards to fill each vacated place; unforeseen accidents hinder intentions, and old plans are forgotten"[2] That is to say, reason should triumph over passion.

There are numerous instances of Time's destruction of love and beauty in Hardy's short stories. The heroine of "Barbara, of the House of Grebe", grows estranged from her husband: "In the meantime the young married lovers, caring no more about their blood than about ditch-water, were intensely happy—happy, that is, in the descending scale which, as we all know, Heaven in its wisdom has ordained for such rash cases; that is to say, the first week they were in the seventh heaven, the second in the sixth, the third week temperate, the fourth reflective, and so on; a lover's heart after possession being comparable to the earth in its geologic stages . . . , first a hot coal, then a warm one, then cooling cinder, then chilly—the simile shall be pursued no further."[3] Other changes similar to this are found in this same group of stories. Dornell's daughter, Betty, who is to be "The First Countess of Wessex", has married Reynaud, a favorite of her mother's. The girl cares more for a worthless lover, Charles, than for her husband, but the latter predicts that Time will cure

[1] *Collected Poems*, p. 212, from "Time's Laughingstocks."
[2] *Tess*, p. 280.
[3] *A Group of Noble Dames*, p. 61.

her of her fickleness: "In twelve months his girl-wife's recent infatuation might be as distasteful to her mind as it was now to his own. In a few years her very flesh would change—so said the scientific; her spirit so much more ephemeral, was capable of changing in one."[1]

Time is equally cruel to "The Marchioness of Stonehenge", who had unwisely wed a man beneath her in a thoughtless moment. "Towards the latter part of the month, when the first wild warmth of her love had gone off, the Lady Caroline sometimes wondered within herself how she, who might have chosen a peer of the realm, baronet, knight—or, if serious-minded, a bishop or judge of the more gallant sort who prefer young wives—could have brought herself to do a thing so rash as to make this marriage."[2]

Of "The Honourable Laura", Hardy says: "To say that her beauty quite departed as the years rolled on would be to over-state the truth. Time is not a merciful master, as we all know, and he was not likely to act exceptionally in the case of a woman who had mental troubles to bear in addition to the ordinary weight of years."[3] Time is so cruel to Viviette's beauty that when Swithin returns to her on the Tower, he is shocked at the ravages of Time and she, seeing his disappointment, dies in his arms.[4] In *The Well Beloved* it is suggested that Jocelyn is cursed by a recurrence of the tender passion every twenty years. Such absurd uses of Time in this book are typical of its lack of excellence.

Time does not confine its activities to the wrecking of love and beauty. It sometimes brings disillusion with all of nature itself. An example of this motif is "To Outer Nature."[5] Everything worth while—truth, joy, love, and faith is destroyed by disillusion in "Memory and I."[6] Time has blighted them all. Time's decrees must not be opposed as is shown in "The Clock of the Years." "It was your choice to mar the ordained."[7] His wish

---

[1]*A Group of Noble Dames*, p. 43
[2]*A Group of Noble Dames*, p. 97
[3]*A Group of Noble Dames*, p. 232
[4]*Two on a Tower*, p. 313
[5]*Collected Poems*, p. 54, from "Wessex Poems."
[6]*Collected Poems*, p. 170, from "Poems of the Past and Present."
[7]*Collected Poems*, p. 497, from "Moments of Vision."

for Time to roll back brings his dead love to him, but she changes back to nothingness.

The Time motif occurs again in the sense of unity of all Time. The best example of it is the poem, "Rome: Building a New Street in the Ancient Quarter." In "Time's Central City" Time plays havoc with man's efforts.[1] In "In a Museum," Time itself is timeless:

> "Such a dream is Time that the coo of this ancient bird
> Has perished not, but is blent, or will be blending
> Mid visionless wilds of space with the voice that I heard
> In the full-fuged song of the universe unending."[2]

But "Time is a mock", we are told, in "The Absolute Explains."

> "Yet hath he been believed in much,
> Though lately, under stress
> Of science less."[3]

But Hardy stands aloof and views the endless extent of years as does the noble Matterhorn which he describes:

> "Saw'st maybe, Joshua's pausing sun and moon,
> And the betokening sky when Caesar's power
> Approached its bloody end; yea, even that noon
> When darkness filled the earth till the ninth hour."[4]

In Hardy, Time takes on a new significance as a motif for art, a fatal sway over the lives of men that gives it even vague personality and an awe-inspiring immanence in things. The endlessness of Time and its effect upon the trivial existence of humanity is set off in contrast to the great consequences that may be inherent in the slightest moment. Time is an arch-instrument of Fate, but as such it operates within the bounds of credibility and as a powerful aid to distinction in Hardy's works.

---

[1] *Collected Poems*, p. 93, from "Poems of the Past and Present."
[2] *Collected Poems*, p. 404, from "Moments of Vision."
[3] *Collected Poems*, p. 720, from "Human Shows; Far Phantasies."
[4] *Collected Poems*, p. 97, from "Poems of the Past and Present."

CHAPTER V

NATURE

Hardy's conception of the Immanent Will is manifested very clearly through his pantheistic interpretation of Nature. He often seems to have used personified Nature as a synonym for the actual Will. When he writes in his first volume of poetry of "Nature's trick of birth", he obviously has in mind the force immanent in things, and not Nature in any specific sense.[1] The unity of sentient life impressed him from his youth, and he early extended the idea to the personification of material Nature. The Will revealed in *The Dynasts* is seen elsewhere in the dress of Nature. It appears as a huge expanse of space, hand in hand with the endless extent of time.

Hardy is a master in giving anthropomorphic existence to cosmic matter and in endowing it with powerful moods. Upon Nature he has conferred his own condition of mind, and in his writing it performs in a fatalistic manner typical of his actors. There is, I think, a very definite joining of humanity and environment in his prose that lends it a transcendent epic quality. In this quality Nature seems to be the central force. Rain, trees, ruined castles, and rivers take on a real personality; men assume a nature that is almost that of a god and a human being combined. Natural forces are linked together by a unity of sympathy and influence, and work out their problems by a kind of osmosis. Hardy is replying to the charge of a mechanistic conception of the universe. In the following excerpt one can feel the actual presence of Nature: "The season developed and matured. Another year's instalment of flowers, leaves, nightingales, thrushes, finches, and other creatures, took up their positions where only a year ago others had stood in their place, and they were nothing more than germs and inorganic particles. Rays from the sunrise drew forth the buds and stretched them into long stalks, lifted up sap in noiseless

---

[1]*Collected Poems*, p. 58, from "To a Motherless Child."

streams, opened petals, and brought out scents in invisible jets and breathings."[1]   Then again: "In the twilight of the morning, light seems active, darkness passive; in the twilight of evening it is the darkness which is active and crescent, and the light which is the drowsy reverse."[2]

It is not surprising that Hardy seems closest to Nature in her moods of twilight.   Frequently his sky of midday has a touch of greyness, a kind of leaden quality which haunts his vision. For him Nature is usually brooding, not rejoicing; weeping, not smiling.   His conception of it is grotesque in its vastness.   It is alive with mocking shadows.   Its very breath is loaded with hate. It lies in wait in ancient places where Hardy's heroes and heroines frequently meet—in Stonehenge, in the old amphi- theatre of Casterbridge, or near the "Ancient Earthwork."[3] Seldom is Nature in her gayest mood.   In the following passage notice how Nature appears as a sinister personality: "The night came in, and took up its place there, unconcerned and indifferent; the night which had already swallowed up his happi- ness, and was now digesting it listlessly; and was ready to swallow up the happiness of a thousand other people with as little disturb- ance or change of mien."[4]

The various moods of Nature in Hardy appear so completely in unison with the trend of action of his people that it becomes difficult to tell whether Nature is in sympathy with human actions or whether these actions are not forced to reflect the mood of their environment as a part of natural change.   At any rate, those actors who are most in harmony with their environment are usually most contented.   Since Hardy is largely interested in open, out-of-doors Nature, he has more sympathy for those simple, close-to-the-soil characters than he has for the highly rebellious, sophisticated ones.   He plainly shows partiality to rustic men who accept Nature as it is.   Dick Dewey, Gabriel Oak, Diggory Ven, Giles Winterbourne, Clym Yeobright, Marty South, and Tess, to mention only a few, take solace and joy from

---

[1] *Tess*, p. 144
[2] *Tess*, p. 145-146
[3] *A Changed Man*, p. 169
[4] *Tess*, p. 268

the natural life about them. Such close relation does not always mean happiness, but it does carry with it a kind of transcendent peace, a joyous submission and a dislike for too high ambition. Eustacia, Wildeve, Fitzpiers, and others show the inherent sorrows which come from rebellion against environment. Eustacia lives a rebel to Egdon Heath, and is so completely defeated that she escapes only by suicide. Hardy's deep love of Nature perhaps goes far to redeem his conceptions of it from hopeless pessimism.

There are many examples in Hardy's works where Nature is in sympathy with human actions. Sometimes he begins a chapter by setting before us the landscape, the weather, and seasonal changes, to prepare us for what is to come later on in the story. The *Return of the Native*, with its famous first chapter, *Far From the Madding Crowd* and *The Woodlanders* are good examples. Recall Gile's sympathy with inanimate Nature as he and Marty South are planting the fir trees: "Winterbourne's fingers were endowed with a gentle conjuror's touch in spreading the roots of each little tree, resulting in a sort of caress, under which the delicate fibres all laid themselves out in their proper directions for growth. He put most of these roots toward the south-west; for he said, in forty years' time, when some great gale is blowing from that quarter, the trees will require the strongest holdfast on that side to stand against it and not fall. 'How they sigh directly we put 'em upright, though while they are lying down, they don't sigh at all', added Marty. She erected one of the young pines into its hole, and held up her finger; the soft musical breathing instantly set in which was not to cease night or day till the grown tree should be felled—probably long after the two planters had been felled themselves. 'It seems to me', Marty continued, 'as if they sigh because they are very sorry to begin life in earnest—just as we be.' "[1]

In some verses called "The Pine Planters", the same idea is expressed.[2]

After Paula's refusal of De Stancey in *A Laodicean*, the ancient De Stancey castle burns, and there appears a symbolism behind the old pile of stone as it is consumed: "The flame increased,

[1]*The Woodlanders*, p. 64
[2]*Collected Poems*, p. 255, from "Time's Laughingstocks".

and . . . roared around the pictures, the tapestries, and the cradle, up to the plaster ceiling and through it into the forest of oak timbers above."[1] Flames are more definitely anthropomorphized in this passage: "The fire glanced up on Paula, and Paula glanced down at the fire."[2]

In the furious storm which accompanies the death of Wildeve and Eustacia, and later on in the death of Giles, we catch the sympathy of Nature. It is in a storm, too, that Jocelyn and Marcia conceive a ruinous passion for each other.[3] Nature shows her wrath and indignation by sending a terrific thunderstorm just after Troy's drunken spree has ended. The starvation of her soul is suggested by "The Starve-acre place" where Tess goes to labor after Clare deserts her. The idyllic landscape of *Under The Greenwood Tree* and *The Trumpet Major*, also harmonizes with the spirit of Nature.

We read, in "The Waiting Supper", that "The waterfall hissed sarcastically of the inevitableness of the unpleasant."[4] The ashes of Eustacia's love for Wildeve are suggested by the ashes of the bonfire.[5] The wind sighs mournfully when sorrow threatens *Tess*: "The occasional heave of the wind became the sigh of some immense sad soul, conterminous with the universe in space, and with history in time."[6] At other times Nature cannot so easily reflect the moods of its people: "July passed over their heads, and the Thermidorean weather which came in its wake seemed an effort on the part of Nature to match the state of hearts at Talbothay's Dairy."[7] In these instances of Nature a kind of Coincidence as well as Fate is manifested. Though they are fatalistic, they are not fatal. They are more of a basic motif in which Nature does not participate, and are therefore, hardly instruments of Fate.

Growing out of this idea is an interpretation of man's relation to Nature parallel to his relation to Time. Hardy is not un-

---

[1] *A Laodicean*, p. 476
[2] *A Laodicean*, p. 210
[3] *The Well Beloved*, p. 25
[4] *A Changed Man*, p. 52
[5] *The Return of the Native*, p. 226
[6] *Tess*, p. 31
[7] *Tess*, p. 166

naturally impressed with the insignificance of man in such a cosmic system, in a timeless Nature which seems to swallow up his pretensions to individuality. Sometimes, however, he does feel a certain sympathy for man, and often sees through man's eye how powerful an instrument Nature can be in one's life. This attitude is perfectly consistent with his system. We have seen that Hardy, as well as Schopenhauer, teaches that the very immanence of the Will invites conflict among its separate manifestations. All possess the Will to live and such a struggle for existence is bound to bring war and turmoil. The pig must lose its life that Arabella and Jude might live. Hardy is more interested in man that he is in animals, yet he was concerned with the movement against cruelty to dumb animals. To him Nature's laws are often mere butchery forced upon man by Fate.

Nature as a conscious agent, usually for evil, is often found in Hardy's works. In this capacity it moves to further the inevitable trend of events—inevitable at least in his mature works where a system of Determinism operates. Its chief function is to show us man's defenseless condition before the devices of Fate. It may take as many forms as Nature itself, or it may be only a momentary interference or an encompassing influence.

The best known example of this last mentioned type is the influence exerted by Egdon Heath in shaping the destiny of its people. Hardy never surpasses this personification of Fate and its effects in terms of natural phenomena. The people of this barren heath are ruled by it, and finally crushed by it. Through its sinister influence Mrs. Yeobright, Eustacia, Wildeve, and Clym all meet death. In such a place only the Reddleman and Thomasin can be halfway happy—chiefly because they belong to it and do not rebel against it. With a soulless cruelty it punishes aliens without mercy. This is the real force of the story—this terrible space of barren land, so sad that it "wore the appearance of an instalment of night which had come to take its place before its astronomical hour has come . . . The spot was, indeed, a near relation of night, and when night showed itself an apparent tendency to gravitate together could be perceived in its shades and the scene . . . Every night its Titanic form seemed to await something . . . The storm was its lover, and the wind its friend . . . as with some persons who have long lived apart, solitude seemed to look out of its countenance. It had a lonely face, suggesting tragical possibilities."[1] It is evident that Hardy considered Egdon Heath a personality, and likewise thought of it as an agent of Fate. It was a tentacle of the Immanent Will whose business it was to crush the desires of its people.

A softer mood of Nature is reflected in Blackmoor Vale, but it controls the destinies of *The Woodlanders*. In this novel an old tree holds in its clutches the destinies of several people, and when these same people cut it down, it wreaks its vengeance upon them. When the tree is no more, the old man, Marty's father, dies, leaving Giles a pauper by means of a peculiar phrase in the property lease. Without a home Giles cannot marry Grace, and she turns to Fitzpiers, marries him, realizes that she still loves Giles, and is consequently doomed to a tragic life with Fitzpiers. All could have been averted had the old tree been left standing. The tree was felled for "the best", but "the worst" came of it.

In many of the early novels, the Nature motif of Fate is used. The unsuspecting Cytherea, of *Desperate Remedies*, is first put into Manston's power by a thunder-storm. Hardy personifies the storm vaguely: "Livid grey shades made a mystery of the remote and dark parts of the vista, and seemed to insist upon a suspension of breath."[2] He describes the fire which destroys the elder Springrove's tavern and says that "the continuance of this quiet process is throughout its length at the mercy of one particular whim of Nature: that is, a sudden breeze."[3] Again, "Nature does few things directly. A minute later an ignited fragment fell on the straw."[4]

A significant motif of this kind is that splendid scene in *A Pair of Blue Eyes* in which Henry Knight hangs over the cliff "Without a Name." The cliff possesses a hostile personality. Hardy describes it: "It is with cliffs and mountains as with persons;

---

[1]*The Return of the Native*, pp. 3-6
[2]*Desperate Remedies*, p. 148
[3]*Ibid.*, P. 193
[4]*Ibid.*, p. 195

they have what is called a presence, which is not necessarily proportionate to their actual bulk. A little cliff will impress you powerfully; a great one not at all. It depends as with man, upon the countenance of the cliff. 'I cannot bear to look at that cliff,' said Elfride. 'It has a horrid personality, and makes me shudder!' 'Can you climb?' said Knight. 'If so, we will ascend by that path over the grim old fellow's brow'."[1] Knight's escape leads to their declaring their love for each other. At that very moment Stephen Smith is sailing into the harbor to claim her for his own.

Just as Nature dominates *The Woodlanders*, so it does *Far From the Madding Crowd*. Gabriel comes back into Bathsheba's life because of the straw rick fire. Otherwise, he would have passed by her farm in search of another position. Again, they come together while trying to save the wheat and barley stacks from the rain. Then there is that hideously grotesque trick that Nature plays on Troy when the heavy rain through the gurgoyle uproots his flowers on Fanny's grave.

In *The Hand of Ethelberta* Sol and Chickerel cannot land in time to prevent the heroine's wedding. Hardy personifies the wind in *Two on a Tower* when it tears off part of Swithin's workshop: "Himself now calmed and satisfied, Swithin, as is the wont of humanity, took serener views of Nature's crushing mechanics without, and said, 'The wind doesn't seem disposed to put the tragic period to our hopes and fears that I spoke of in my momentary despair.' 'The disposition of the wind is as vicious as ever', she answered . . . and, as if flatly to stultify Swithin's assumption, a circular hurricane, exceeding in violence any that had preceded it, seized hold upon Rings-Hill Speer at that moment with the determination of a conscious agent . . . Then the wind, which hitherto they had heard rather than felt, rubbed past them like a fugitive."[2] According to Hardy's own words his purpose in writing this novel was "to set the emotional history of the two infinitesimal lives against the stupendous background of the stellar universe." In its pages we get a vivid

---

[1] *A Pair of Blue Eyes*, p. 232
[2] *Two on a Tower*, p. 120

picture of man's insignificance, but this feature does not lessen the author's interest in the human race.

The catastrophes which Michael Henchard received at the hand of Nature are Fate's rewards for his indiscretions and bitter thoughts. Nature sees to it that his schemes to ruin Farfrae fail. Not only does the rain spoil his celebration, but it actually enhances Farfrae's. Nature plays peculiar tricks on Henchard, who accepts the prediction of a local seer, buys great stocks of grain, and has to sell at a loss because the weather and the weather prophet did not agree.

We see these Nature motifs in Hardy's verse as well as in his prose. "Proud Songsters" reminds us that all Nature is one, for just one year before these little birds were only particles of earth, air and rain. In "Suspense" the personality is reflected:

> "A clamminess hangs over all like a clout,
> The fields are a water-colour washed out . . .
> The sky will look the same thereupon,
> And the wind and the sea go groaning on."[1]

A tree assumes a definitely anthropomorphic nature and falls in love with a lady in "The Tree and the Lady."[2] In "August Midnight"[3] and "The Last Chrysanthemum"[4], he insists that rustic creatures know best Nature's secrets. Nature appears herself in "The Mother Mourns":

> "Weary plaint that Mankind, in these late days,
>   Had grieved her by holding
> Her ancient high fame of perfection
>   In doubt and disdain."[5]

In employing the Nature motif in his works, Hardy used it with affection and understanding. He felt at home in the great out-of-doors, and he interpreted it only as one could who had dealt long and thoughtfully with it.

---

[1]*Winter Words*, p. 124
[2]*Collected Poems*, p. 499, from "Moments of Vision"
[3]*Collected Poems*, p. 134, from "Poems of the Past and the Present"
[4]*Collected Poems*, p. 137, from "Poems of the Past and the Present"
[5]*Collected Poems*, p. 101, from "Poems of the Past and the Present"

CHAPTER VI

WOMAN

The characters of Hardy's novels tend to fall into groups. They may, in a general sense, be said to run to types, perhaps because his observation of humanity was impressed with the similarities of people in a common predicament. He divided the human race two ways: by motive and by sex, like the four points of a compass. The verticle points separated the male from the female; the horizontal, the good from the bad. But in Hardy's deterministic system badness seems to have no very real significance as distinct from goodness. Humanity is composed of bits and ends of the Immanent Will; therefore, they have no responsibility and cannot be condemned. The real division then, lies between two groups: those who, like Hardy, consider it wise to seek truth and goodness, resignedly hoping for no reward; and those who do not. He considers this latter group less responsible than the one to which he belongs. I do not mean to infer that resignation and irresponsibility are synonymous terms with Hardy. The genuine criterion is in the presence or absence of nobility.

All of these groups appear in the novels. Between such characters as Clym Yeobright, Diggory Venn, Gabriel Oak, Giles Winterbourne, and Jude Fawley on one side, and Sergeant Troy, Wildeve, Dr. Fitzpiers and Alex D'Urberville on the other, there is a clear line of demarcation. The same difference is to be seen between the two groups of women: Thomasin, Marty South, Elizabeth-Jane, and Tess on one side, with Elfride, Ethelberta, Eustacia and Arabella on the other. None of these people are determinedly vicious or bad. There is much that is noble in each of them, more than that which is usually in evidence. The trouble arises in that they refuse to cultivate this finer side, and allow their primitive instincts to get control and run on unrestrained. They do not possess that balance, so necessary in life, which comes from a persistent devotion to goodness.

The broad distinction between masculine and feminine temperament is quite important in Hardy's conception of character.
He considers them to be as divergent, in some respects, as animals
of different species. They respond to the same basic situations
in entirely different ways. Indeed, they are "the two halves
intended by Nature to make the perfect whole."[1] They supplement each other, however, in that each lends to the other certain
qualities lacking in their makeup. Soon after Hardy's books
began to appear, many critics, especially women, accused him of
attempting to calumniate the female sex. Most of them knew
and cared nothing about his theories of philosophy, and those
who did could not see in it sufficient grounds for such an attitude.
Yet we can hope to understand his representation of Woman
only through his approach to her as an instrument of Fate. Hardy
did not detest Woman at all; he simply saw in her nature one of
the several sources from which man derives much of his misery.

Charles Lamb once remarked that Shakespeare had no male
heroes in his plays; all of his heroes were of the other sex. This
is not true in Hardy's works, yet he does unify his action around
a central figure, usually a woman. We need not be surprised at
this, for in a man-made world, Woman naturally assumes the
most interesting position for him. Hardy sees the universe
through the eyes of a man. His attitude is not that reflected in
Meredith's flattering treatment of womanhood, nor is it that
of the sworn hostility of Strindberg. It is the analytical, disinterested scrutiny of a person who stands aloof, who can prevent
his head from following his heart, who is strongly fascinated by
Woman, but is able to preserve a sane mental equilibrium. He
regrets the domination of sex in man, because it makes him such
an easy prey for the fateful lure of the woman.

This accounts for Hardy's method of having his main action
center around a woman character in most instances and at the
same time causing the reader's sympathies to rest with a man
under her domination. Frequently the heroine has two or more
lovers at the same time, but the author concentrates our attention
upon a certain one of them. Fancy Day is the heroine of *Under*

---

[1]The History of the Hardcombes", in *Life's Little Ironies*, p. 214-215

The Greenwood Tree, but attention goes largely to Dick Dewey. In *Far From the Madding Crowd* it is Bathsheba who dominates the story, yet we are concerned with and extend our sympathies to that paragon of virtue, Gabriel Oak. Eustacia Vye and Clym Yeobright offer a better example still. The fickle Anne Garland of *The Trumpet Major* has two brother lovers, but the one she gets concerns us little compared with the one she loses. Somerset's happiness is of more interest to us than is that of Paula, the truly "Laodicean". We instinctively feel satisfied with the defeat of Viviette in *Two on a Tower*, because we think it will allow Swithin to complete his ambitious studies. In *The Woodlanders* Giles commands our sympathies, yet the action centers about Grace Melbury. *Tess* and *The Hand of Ethelberta* are possible exceptions to this classification. In the latter novel Ethelberta is the center of our attention, but we are glad to see Julian marry Picotee and not her less worthy sister. We feel most concern for these central characters in those three novels where the hero is obviously the man. This is true of Michael Henchard, Jude Fawley, and Jocelyn Pierston of *The Well Beloved.*

When Hardy first describes Eustacia Vye in *The Native* he attaches a peculiar significance to the consideration of Woman as an agent of Fate. He seems to identify her nature clearly with that of the Immanent Will: "Eustacia Vye was the raw material of a Divinity. On Olympus she would have done well with a little preparation . . . Had it been possible for the earth and mankind to be entirely in her grasp for a while, had she handled the distaff, the spindle, and the shears at her own free-will, few in the world would have noticed the change of government. There would have been the same inequality of lot, the same heaping up of favors here, of contumely there, the same generosity before justice, the same perpetual dilemmas, the same captious interchange of blows, as those we endure now."[1] Since Eustacia is one of the most typical of all Hardy's women, this description is very significant. She was "not quite a faultless woman", because she did not follow after the good so consistently as did Marty South. Neither was she intentionally bad. We

---

[1] *The Return of The Native*, p. 75

fully accept her lament at the end of the story: "How I have tried and tried and tried to be a splendid woman!" She has proved to be a typical Hardy heroine, neither good nor bad, with immense potentialities for both.

▪ Hardy maintains that Woman is more irresponsible, more a slave to primitive feelings than Man. Since Woman's chief business is to find Man to support her she becomes an agent in his destiny. Of all Fate's instruments for opposing man's happiness, she is the most potent. She becomes Nature's symbol, closer to the primitive energy than Man.

Man is not so much concerned with love as is Woman. For him it is a pastime; for her it is of deep concern. Her whole life is given to securing the best mate she can. Love is her game, her joy, and the motivating passion of her life. For her, love is "a will, not a latent force." She has become the positive entity in sexual relations; man is the negative. At least this is Hardy's opinion as he indicates many times. In his opening description of Clym and Eustacia, we get a contrast of the parts Woman and Man are doomed to play in matters of love. Man, although he retains many fundamental passions, has been moved by modern forces; but woman has resisted them and clings to her basic instincts.

Sex relations constitute a conflict which can be explained only on the basis of a contact between the philosophy of Hardy and that of Schopenhauer. This, we have seen, is at the base of all Nature which is endowed with the Will to be. Now, since Woman's chief purpose in life is to live and be sustained, she bends every effort to secure Man as sustainer. Who could doubt such a philosophy in the case of Arabella and Jude? The battle of Man against Woman has gone on for ages, just as inevitably as the struggle between Egdon Heath and its people. Fate has marked the cards against Man in that he is endowed with an irresistible instinct for her charms. The aces and kings are all in Woman's hand in this fascinating but ruinous game. Man cannot play at chess; whist is the game.

But Hardy does not say that instinct is responsible for the tragedy of love. Love itself is not a tragedy; but it is the quality which Woman possesses which makes it so. Woman must

possess Man.   Often it is by seduction, deception and her innocent
charms.   Recall Arabella's ability to make her dimples appear on
a second's notice whenever Jude came into view.   When Eustacia
dons boy's attire to act the Moor in the St. George Play, when
Viviette sets out to capture the youthful astronomer, and when
Arabella adopts the disgusting method of attracting Jude's
attention, the fly walks into the web, but the web has been
carefully spun.

Frequently Woman employs Law and Convention to catch
her game.   Marriage brings her protection and dignity.   Arabella
sums it up: "Life with a man is more business-like after (marriage) and money matters work better.   And then, you see, if
you have rows and he turns you out of doors, you can get the
law to protect you, which you can't otherwise, unless he half
runs you through with a knife or cracks your noddle with a
poker.   And if he bolts away from you . . . you'll have the
sticks o' furniture, and wont be looked upon as a thief."[1]   While
Woman calls upon Law and Convention to aid her, she is hostile
to both.   She is chagrined to find herself a slave to them, that
her very life depends upon their decrees and statutes.   They
stand ready to crush her at any moment; yet better to effect
Man's doom, they join hands with her and thus become joint
instruments of Fate.

Biological urge or sustenance is not always the source of Woman's strife to possess Man.   The biological urge is absent when
Ethelberta snares Lord Mountclere, and when Viviette tricks
the Bishop of Manchester into marrying her.   The desire for
sustenance is often lacking, for many of Hardy's heroines are
women of wealth.   Bathsheba's acceptance of Oak, Paula's
enticing of Somerset, Viviette's capturing of Swithin are all
instances where money was not the object.   In these cases we
see another object, or force at work—where wealthy women
throw themselves in the paths of poor youths of humble parentage
and regret it forever after.   This temperament of Woman which
works as a means to ruin Man's happiness is a complicated affair
and we shall try to see how it operates as an arm of Fate.

---

[1] *Jude*, p. 318

While Hardy's women are not by any means all alike, they do possess qualities common to their sex, and which he thought necessary to every woman's nature. Among these he rated unrestrained passion—with its chief supplement, indecision— very high. Now neither of these is an evil, but when operating in unison, brings man untold woe. "Mere vessel of emotions", he calls Tess, and the epithet might be applied to many of his Tesses.[1] Logic plays little part in their actions. At heart they are animals, whose chief charm is physical beauty, used to entice man. Hardy actually speaks of many of them as animals: Eustacia is a "crying animal", Picotee, an "unreasoning animal", and Arabella is a "female animal". Of an unimportant heroine he says: "That he had been able to seduce another woman in two days was his crowning though unrecognized fascination for her as the she-animal."[2]

Woman's emotion fills Hardy's pages. "Elfride's emotion was cumulative and after awhile would assert itself on a sudden. A slight touch was enough to set it free—a poem, a sunset, a cunningly contrived chord of music, a vague imagining."[3] A similar emotionalism is found in Cytherea Graye: "The touch of clothes, which was nothing to Manston, sent a thrill through Cytherea, seeing moreover that he was of the nature of a mysterious stranger."[4] She says of her reaction to love that "the emotion I felt made me forgetful of realities."[5]

Music and dancing have a delirious influence on Hardy's women. Cytherea is overcome by Manston's organ playing, and soon submits to his love entreaties. It is at an open air dance that Wildeve recaptures Eustacia's heart after she had married Clym. In "The History of the Hardcombes" music plays havoc with four lovers, who are so acted upon by emotion that they marry the wrong cross partners, only to realize the error when it is too late.[6] Poor Car'line cannot resist Ollamoor, "The Fiddler of the Reels", when he fiddles, although she despises him at all

---

[1]*Tess*, p. 11
[2]"On the Western Circuit", from *Life's Little Ironies*, p. 125
[3]*A Pair of Blue Eyes*, p. 214
[4]*Desperate Remedies*, p. 151
[5]*Ibid.*, p. 242
[6]*Life's Little Ironies*

other times.[1] This overpowering influence of dance music is also seen in his poetry.[2]

Obviously, Woman is not to blame for this emotional reaction to music. She is part of a deterministic system which can use her to advantage in this state. Hardy says of the milk maids at Talbothays Dairy, who had fallen in love with Clare: "They writhed feverishly under the oppressiveness of an emotion thrust on them by cruel Nature's law—an emotion which they had neither expected nor desired."[3]

Hardy's women cannot escape this emotion; for them it spells sadness. As cool and well balanced as Bathsheba is, she cannot resist the power of Troy's trim uniform and shining sword. All of her relations with him proved tragic. That same uniform had lured Fanny Robin too, and by it she had been brought to a dishonorable end. John Loveday loses Anne Garland because the uniform of his worthless brother was too much for her emotional mind to resist.

This unbridled passion is usually accompanied by instability of temperament. Women are fickle by nature and change their minds without provocation. They respond quickly to impulses and act thereupon without the correction of reason.

It is the combination of these characteristics that most often destroys Man. Helpless herself in the hands of Fate, Woman acts as agent for Fate in carrying out its work with Man.

Cytherea Graye of *Desperate Remedies* seems to be the first of this volatile group. Although she and Springrove declare their love early in the story, yet their relations are consistently uncertain. Her obligations to her ill brother and to Miss Henton, however, may partially excuse her instability. Even Fancy Day suffers from the indecision characteristic of her sex. Promised and ready to wed Dick Dewey, she is swept off her feet by Maybold, agrees to marry him, and then at his suggestion, she accepts Dick.

Elfride Swancourt, one of Hardy's typical heroines, comes forth with one of her most positive characteristics: "Woman's ruling passion—to fascinate and rule those more powerful than

---

[1]*Life's Little Ironies*, p. 180
[2]*Collected Poems*, "The Fiddler"
[3]*Tess*, p. 187

she—though operant in Elfride, was decidedly purposeless."[1] And so it was, for this fickle girl, lovable in spite of her faults, for she is not responsible for them, leads astray four men, one of whom dies for her, and another of whom buries her. Bathsheba Everdene is a prime example of fickleness in woman. She rules two good men to their sorrow, and finally submits to a worthless one. When she chose Troy and refused Oak and Boldwood, she demonstrated a lack of judgment rare even in Hardy's heroines. It was through no evil intent that she sent that valentine to Boldwood, yet it started a chain of events which Fate used to ruin him through the disguise of a woman.

Ethelberta is one of the lot who was not dominated by passion. Her intentions are always good: to support a large family; but, by doing this, she brings grief to four men, one of whom she marries. Her greatest sin was trifling with Julian's affections. Eustacia seems most culpable of all the heroines, but Fate and not evil intention leads her to play with Wildeve and wreck her husband's life. Fancy, Ethelberta, Paula, Grace and Anne Garland all engage in this guilty traffic. The least attractive of these, as well as the most guilty, is Anne Garland. Her only vice is utter irresponsibility.

Not much better is Paula Power who deserts Somerset because the high sounding name De Stancey appeals to her empty ambitious nature. She rings true to herself when she writes to George Somerset: "Remember it is a natural instinct with us women to retain the power of obliging a man to hope, fear, pray, and beseech as long as we think fit, before we confess to a reciprocal affection."[2] Choose any of the women at random and she will be found to have operated unwittingly to the detriment of Man.

These heroines are also characterized by excessive vanity. Even Tess has her share of this quality.[3] Most of them are unduly curious and see no harm in deceit, if there is anything to be gained by it. Deceit suggests a motif which leads unfailingly to tragedy: a woman's secret. They are undecided about telling it, and usually wait until confession leads only to disaster. Had

---

[1] *A Pair of Blue Eyes*, p. 215
[2] *A Laodicean*, p. 302
[3] *Tess*, p. 386

Elfride told Knight sooner of her love affair with Stephen, all would have gone well. Had Tess told Clare of her secret affair with Alec, both, perhaps, would have been spared. Viviette fails to reveal to Parson Torkingham her relations with her husband and confides in Swithin instead. Ethelberta is haunted by the secret of her humble status, and in *Desperate Remedies* Mrs. Aldclyffe is tormented by the secret that Manston is her son. The secret of Elizabeth-Jane's parentage and many others might be enumerated.

Obviously, in the lives of Hardy's men, Woman operates for evil. But she does so not wittingly, but as an instrument, which has endowed her with a volatile nature.

Chapter VII

CONVENTION AND LAW

Up to this point we have considered only those motifs of Fate which have been primary and direct manifestations. In this concluding chapter we shall notice the working of Fate through an artificial form, made at secondhand by those very beings who will be destroyed by it. The motif of Convention was the last one to develop in Hardy's works, but it is of much importance, especially in his last novels. He never elaborated the idea to the extent of the others; but that it operated clearly and fatally is unquestionable.

In attacking Convention so fiercely, Hardy was falling in line with a spirit that was increasing in England at his time. Influence was brought to bear upon it from abroad, especially that of Ibsen's plays. *Tess* belongs to its period just as much as does *The Second Mrs. Tanqueray*, *Lady Windermere's Fan* or *Mrs. Dane's Defence*. But *Tess* has outlived these because it possesses an art which they lack. Of all manifestations of Fate in Hardy, Convention is the most conventional and perhaps the least pleasing.

In all of the earlier cases Man has been helpless and resigned, but here he is in open rebellion and with sufficiently good reasons. When confronted by these other hostile forces, Man has been quite powerless, because they were created by powers beyond his control; but things that are made by Man can be handled by Man and he need not submit to such creations unless he is ignorant and stupid. This is seen clearly in *Tess* and *Jude*— violent pleas against evils which can and ought to be corrected. Obviously they have forgotten the restrictions of determinism.

For Hardy, conventions are "the artificial forms of living."[1] He has no patience with those who hold them to be the "cardinal

---

[1] *Early Life*, p. 279

facts of life." Social law and natural law tend to work in conflict with a destructive effect. We blame the one or the other for our ills, depending on whether we favor the one or the other. Victorians for the most part sided with Convention and condemned Tess; Hardy and a few followers fought for liberty and the triumph of the intellect.

Convention, as it is used here, means all the social customs of the period, set up by general consent, as the institutions, customs, and prejudices—some in the form of statutes, and some existing only in the mind. Hardy was opposed to the abuses inherent in all of these, yet he did not cast his lot with the anarchists. His only objection to Convention was that it conflicted with natural law. He was convinced that the fundamental structure of man's law was sound, for its purpose was to maintain peace and order. But in the many centuries through which it had passed out of its useful sphere and had assumed functions and powers to which it was not entitled, it had built up a system of regulations hostile and burdensome to Man. It was this constant fear of Convention getting absolute control that caused him to direct so much attention to it.

Those reviewers who attacked *Jude* when it appeared made the fundamental error of supposing the laws of marriage and the institution of marriage to be the same thing. Hardy opposed such an interpretation, but by no means did he advocate the abolition of the rite as so many of his enemies maintained. He subjected it to the same test to which he would have subjected any other law of England—when it restrained Man in direct opposition to his higher wishes and better nature, he was opposed to it.

Hardy's objection to marriage of the usual kind was based on the fact that a temporary infatuation for the moment, accompanied by no affinities or compatibilities of any kind, was all that was necessary to constitute a marriage contract. Even a more careful consideration of the suitability of both parties would help but little, for a clear, dispassionate weighing of facts is impossible in matters of love. Perhaps it is impossible for Woman at any time. One moment of passion may destroy a whole lifetime. Jude saw the situation but was unable to meet it: "There seemed to him, vaguely and dimly, something wrong in a social ritual which made necessary a cancelling of well-formed schemes involving years of thought and labour, of foregoing a man's one opportunity of showing himself superior to the lower animals, and of contributing his units of work to the general progress of his generation, because of a momentary surprise by a new and transitory instinct which had nothing in it of the nature of vice, and could only at the most be called weakness."[1]

Instead of marriage being a friend of man, it often takes advantage of him by attacking a temporary weakness. It attempts to turn a passing passion into a life-long contract. Such a system is certain to bring disaster, especially after the physical attraction has lulled. Now, the sorrow of marriage lies in the action of Fate which mates Its people in a hit-or-miss fashion without any attempt to consider their suitability. In doing this It hides behind the man-made laws which aid in carrying out the nefarious business. Again Jude analyzes the situation: "People go on marrying because they can't resist natural forces, although many of them may know perfectly well that they are possibly buying a month's pleasure with a life's discomfort."[2] Man often rebels at the very command to love which is embodied in the ceremony, so perverse is his nature. "It is foreign to man's nature to go on loving a person when he is told that he must and shall be that person's lover. There would be a much likelier chance of his doing it if he were told not to love. If the marriage ceremony consisted in an oath and signed contract between the parties to cease loving from that day forward, in consideration of personal possession being given, and to avoid each other's society as much as possible in public, there would be more loving couples than there are now. Fancy the secret meetings between the perjuring husband and wife, the denials of having seen each other, the clambering in at bedroom windows, and the hiding in closets! There'd be little cooling then."[3] This innate dislike of marriage is seen in the poem, "The Christening":

---

[1] *Jude*, p. 67
[2] *Jude*, p. 306
[3] *Jude*, p. 306

" . . . But chained and doomed for life
    To slovening
As vulgar man and wife,
He says, is another thing
Yea: sweet Love's sepulchring."[1]

When a minor character speaks of the "tragedy of marriage,
full of crimes and catastrophes," which "ends with the death of
one of the actors,"[2] Hardy is not attacking the institution of
marriage, but the loose acceptance of the rite which Man's instincts
make inevitable.   Mutual concessions are necessary if marriage
is to succeed.   The ceremony becomes a symbol of the irrevocable,
for divorce was not such an easy matter in Hardy's day.   We
remember in *The Woodlanders* how impossible it was for Grace
to get a divorce from Fitzpiers.   Sue Bridehead had a horror of
this rite, yet she feels keenly its binding nature for she returns
to Phillotson even after separating from him as she feels that
even lawful divorce cannot dissolve the chain.

Hardy opposed these rigid interpretations of marriage with a
well formed plan.   Sue reminds us of it on two occasions: "I
have been thinking . . . that the social moulds civilization fits
us into have no more relation to our actual shapes than the conventional shapes of the constellation have to the real star-pat-
tern.' "[2]   "Domestic laws should be made according to tempera-
ments, which should be classified.   If people are at all peculiar
in character, they have to suffer from the very rules that produce
comfort in others.' "[4]   More liberal law was the only solution
for such conditions.   Hardy's criticism here seems to hinge on
his hostility to mob spirit and an insistence that the demands
of the individual temperament be considered.   If divorce were
easier, no more careless marriage would be performed than in
our present system.   Then the individual could partially escape
a situation for which he was only in part responsible.

Hardy's opposition to marriage laws was only one aspect of a
general attack of conventional ideas of morality which bring man

---

[1] *Collected Poems*, p. 245
[2] "The Waiting Supper", in *A Changed Man*, p. 39
[3] *Jude*, p. 242
[4] *Jude*, p. 264

to grief. In *Tess* we get a good example of it. It is in Angel Clare's narrow conception of chastity, and his attitude toward convention in general. He is not to blame for the tragedy any more than Tess or Alec D'Urberville. He is simply a victim of Fate which has played so tragically with Tess. He has inherited his ideas from his parents, products of a conservative England. This view of morality, for such a normal man as he, was not to be avoided, but Hardy says society can outgrow it if she will. Clare can improve upon his conception of morality. He fights against his prejudices: He "was incensed against his Fate, bitterly disposed toward social ordinances, for they had cooped him up in a corner, out of which there was no legitimate pathway."[1] Even Tess does not escape the conventional idea of morality. "She might have seen that what had bowed her head so profoundly—the thought of the world's concern at her situation—was founded on an illusion . . . Most of the misery had been generated by her conventional aspect, and not by her innate sensation."[2] But she feels the blight of this tyranny more than Angel: "She was ashamed of herself for her gloom of the night, based on nothing more tangible than a sense of condemnation under an arbitrary law of society which had no foundation in Nature."[3]

Several other conventions are arraigned in Hardy's novels. One that occurs very frequently is that Man should seek to marry on his own social level. Love and marriage in Hardy run foul of any such idea. Family distinction, wealth and education have no effect on the selections of his people. Conventions are not respected, but those who rebel are punished sharply, often from within, for those who refuse to obey conventions believe in them after all. Cytherea Bradleigh and Ambrose Graye of *Desperate Remedies* are Hardy's first loves of social differences. His first unpublished novel, however, bore the title, *The Poor Man and the Lady*. Elfride's father forbids his daughter to associate with Stephen because of his humble birth, and even she is rather alarmed

---

[1] *Tess*, p. 307
[2] *Tess*, p. 100
[3] *Tess*, p. 318

when she learns of it.   In *A Laodicean*, De Stancey has the advantage of Somerset, for he can offer Paula a noble family name, whereas Somerset can offer her nothing but love and honor. Gabriel Oak and Bathsheba Everdene are separated by a social gulf, and so are Grace and Giles, Viviette and Swithin, Tess and Clare.   Many such cases appear in his short stories.   There are a few in the poetry, "A Poor Man and a Lady,"[1] for instance. An example of the haughty and priggish gentleman is found in "The Son's Veto."[2]

Hardy, with no reference to his own case, attacks that conventional system which denies an education to a deserving boy just because he happens to be poor.   Such a Convention joins with Woman and marriage laws to assist Fate in bringing Jude to destruction.

Hardy also objected to the frequent hand taken by legal technicalities in causing suffering to human beings.   Think how often this occurs through the provisions of a marriage license! In the opening of *The Return of the Native*, Thomasin and Wildeve cannot be married in a near by town because their license is not valid in that place.   Similar tricks twist the plot of *Two on a Tower* several times.   Indeed, this story is full of such incidents. When Viviette marries the Bishop, Hardy says that "Convention was forcing her hand at this game; and to what will not Convention compel her weaker victims in extremes?"[3]   "Alicia's Diary" turns on the law that a man cannot wed his wife's sister.[4]

Law often has technicalities of another kind.   Giles was made a pauper by such a technicality in connection with lease-making and holding.   In "Netty Sargent's Copyhold", the heroine outwits such a flaw.[5]   In *Desperate Remedies* Springrove loses his tavern insurance by a flaw in the policies.   This very nearly frustrates the marriage of Edward and Cytherea.   In all of these apparent trifling hitches in the law, the fate of several persons is bound up.

---

[1]*Collected Poems*, p. 759, "Human Shows; Far Phantasies."
[2]*Life's Little Ironies*.
[3]*Two on a Tower*, p. 290.   The early edition, 1895, substitutes "Nature" for "Convention."
[4]*A Changed Man*, etc.
[5]*Life's Little Ironies*

Of all Fate's instruments Convention is the least obvious, because it operates indirectly. It is mob action and opinion for selfish protection, operated at others' expense. It is artificial and kept going by fear. In effect, it is a sort of mold which forms on public opinion, bringing disaster to the individual. It cannot be obliterated completely but it can be directed by enlightenment. By such an admission, Hardy breaks slightly with his system of Determinism which was inevitable.

CONCLUSION

Throughout this study I have attempted to show the influence of Hardy's philosophy of life on the development of his art. Its chief contention has been that it led him to attach particular importance to five motifs of Fate in his verse and prose and to elaborate them in his own way. These motifs occupy positions among the protagonists of the action and guide the destinies of his characters relentlessly.

They are the instruments of Fate in a system of Determinism and become units of a ceaseless machinery. They are manifestations of an Immanent Will, which operates unconsciously and purposelessly through them.

It does not appear that Hardy was fundamentally a philosopher, and his system, which he portrays in *The Dynasts*, as well as in other works, shows defects and inconsistencies to be expected in a poetic representation built on mere fancy. The thoughtful reader will find it difficult to accept the fact that an Unconscious Will can operate consistently for evil when It has no consciousness of either good or evil. We doubt that this Will is as blind as It appears to be, and suspect that often It furtively peers out from Its mask to be sure that all is not right with the world.

This can be explained by remembering that this conception of life evolved out of Hardy's youthful impressions, which were gloomy and pessimistic; and alone they might have led him to believe in the Immanent Will. Although his view of life was extremely pessimistic, in the popular sense at least, he never lost hope that somehow there might be an improvement. In order to reconcile his pessimism and hopefulness, he created his Immanent

Will, unconscious but with powers of sight in the far future.   This helps to explain his inconsistency, but it hardly satisfies.

Thomas Hardy is not a pessimist like Swift, with a skeptic's scorn of humanity.   He is more like Job, who regretted that he had to be born.   The best answer to this predicament is resignation, devotion to Beauty, Truth and Goodness.   We have no control over what is to be our lot, but whatever it is we can face it with magnanimity.   We can live by a code of morality superior to that of the Will.

Hardy, like most determinists, was never able to subject his ideas to a clearly consistent system.   His early belief in Chance breaks out occasionally even after he had accepted Determinism as his guide.   For the most part, however, he believed in idealistic monism.

Taken as a whole, Hardy's works well illustrate a reasonably consistent philosophy of life.   At times it leads him to impose upon credibility and verisimilitude, yet it serves to unify his works and gives them an original and epic character tremendous to contemplate.

BIBLIOGRAPHY

PART I

BOOKS

ABERCROMBIE, LASCELLES; *Thomas Hardy, A Critical Study.* London, 1912.

ARCHER, WILLIAM; *Real Conversations.* Wm. Heinemann, London, 1904.

BEACH, JOSEPH W; *The Technique of Thomas Hardy.* Chicago, 1922.

BERLE, LINA WRIGHT; *Geo. Eliot and Thomas Hardy.* N. Y., 1917.

BITHELL, JETHRO; *Introduction to French Translation of Poems of Thos. Hardy.* 1925.

BLANCHE, JACQUES; *Mes Modeles.* Paris, 1928.

BLAZE DE BURY, Y; *Les Romanciers Anglais Contemporains.* Paris, 1900.

BAZILE, GEORGES; *"Une Femme Imaginative!* Nouvelle traduite de l'anglais,'' Les cahiers britanniques et Americains d'aujourd'hui, No. 2.

BERNARD-DEROSNE, YORICK; *"Le Trompette Major,* Roman traduite de l'anglais.'' Hachette, Paris, 1882.

BOLVIN, MME. H; *"Les Petites Ironies de la Vie,* Nouvelles traduited de l'anglais.'' Rieder, Paris, 2me édition, 1920.

BOUCHER, LÉON; *Le Roman Pastoral en Angleterre.*

BOYD, E. A.; *Literary Blasphemies,* Harpers, 1927.

BRAYBROOK, PATRICK; *Thomas Hardy and His Philosophy.* Phil., 1927.

BREBNER, J. B; *Classics of the Western World.* Chicago, 1927.

BRENNECKE, EARNEST, JR.; *Thomas Hardy's Universe: A Study of a Poet's Mind.* London, 1924.

BROWNE, P. H.; *A Collection of Writings of Thomas Hardy.* Harvard Library, 1927.

BRENNECKE, ERNEST, JR.; *The Life of Thomas Hardy.* New York, 1925.

BRUNIUS, A.; *Ansikter och Masker;* "Thomas Hardy och hans nya diktsamlingar,'' p.p. 36-45.

BURDETT, OSBERT; *The Beardsley Period.* London, 1925.

BURRISS, SARAH LUCILE; *Characters in the Fiction of Thomas Hardy.* Cornell Thesis, pub. in "The Meridith College Quarterly Bulletin,'' series 22, Nos. I to 2, Nov., 1928 and Jan., 1929.

BURTON, RICHARD; *Masters of English Novel.* N. Y., 1909.

CALVERTON, V.; *Sex Expression in Literature.* N. Y., 1926.

CATALOGNE, GIRARD DE; *Le Message de Thomas Hardy.* Paris, 1928.

CAZAMIAN, MADELIENE L.; *Le Roman et les Idées en Angleterre.* Strasbourg, 1923.

CHAPMAN, E. M.; *The Newer Fiction.* 1900.

CHAPMAN, E. M.; *English Literature in Account with Religion. 1800-1900.* N. Y. 1910.

CHASE, MARY ELLEN; *The Well Beloved from Serial to Novel.* Thesis, Minneapolis, 1918.

CHASE, MARY ELLEN; *Thomas Hardy from Serial to Novel.* Minneapolis, 1927, (Annotated copies of *The Mayor of Casterbridge, Tess of the D'Urbervilles,* and *Jude the Obscure,* showing all changes from serial to novel, have been deposited by Miss Chase in the University of Minnesota Library.)

CHESTERTON, G. K.; *The Victorian Age in Literature.* N. Y. 1913.

CHILD, HAROLD H.; *Thomas Hardy.* London, 1916.

CHEVALLEY, ABEL; *Le Roman Anglais de Notre Temps.* London, 1921.

CHEW, SAMUEL C.; *Thomas Hardy, Poet and Novelist.* Bryn Mawr, 1921

COLLINS, VERE H.; *Talks with Thomas Hardy at Max Gate.* Duckworth, London, 1928.

CROSS, W. L.; *Development of the English Novel.* N. Y., 1899.

CUNLIFFE, J. W.; *English Literature During the Last Half Century.* N. Y., 1919, p. p. 40-56.

DANIELSON, HENRY; *The First Editions of the Writings of Thomas Hardy and Their Values.* London, 1916.

DAWSON, WM. J.; *Makers of English Fiction,* pp. 213-240, 1905.

DAWSON, W. J. AND DAWSON, C. W.; *The Great English Novelists.* N. Y. and London, 1911.

DELATTRE, FLORIS; *Dickens et la France.* 1927.

DOBRÉE, BONAMY; *The Lamp and The Lute: Studies of Six Modern Authors,* pp. 21-44 Oxford, 1929.

DUFFIN, H. C.; *Thomas Hardy: A Study of the Wessex Novels.* Manchester, 1916.

ELLWANGER, GEO. H.; *Idyllists of the Country Side.* N. Y., 1895.

ELTON, OLIVER; *Modern Studies.* 1907.

ESDAILE, ARUNDELL; "Bibliography of Thomas Hardy's Principal Works" in Harold Child's *Thomas Hardy.* N. Y., 1916.

EXIDEUIL, PIERRE D'; *Le Couple Humain dans L'Oeuvre de Thomas Hardy.* Paris, 1928.

EXIDEUIL, PIERRE D'; *The Human Pair in The Work of Thomas Hardy*, translated from the French by F. W. Crosse. London, 1930. French edition, 1928. Introduction by Havelock Ellis.

FIROR, RUTH A.; *Folkways in Thomas Hardy.* U. of Penna. Press, Phil., 1931.

FLACCUS, L. W.; *The Spirit of Substance and Art.* Crofts, 1926.

FOGELGUIST, T.; *Typer och Tänkesätt,* 1927.

FOLLET, HELEN AND WILSON; *Some Modern Novelists.* N. Y. 1918.

FOWLER, J. H.; *The Novels of Thomas Hardy.* Oxford Press, 1928. English Assoc., Pamphlet 71.

FREEMAN, JOHN; *The Moderns.* 1916.

FRIERSON, W. C.; *L'Influence du Naturalism Francais sur les Romanciers Anglais de 1885 à 1900.* Paris, 1925.

FRYE, P. H.; *Literary Reviews,* pp. 104-113.

GARDNER, W. H.; "Some Thoughts on *The Mayor of Casterbridge.*" English Assoc. Pamphlet 77, Nov. 1930.

GARWOOD, HELEN; *Thomas Hardy: An Illustration of the Philosophy of Schopen-hauer.* U. of Penna. Thesis, Phila., 1911.

GOSSE, EDMUND; *Some Diversions of A Man of Letters.* "The Lyrical Poetry of Thomas Hardy." London.

GRIMSDITCH, H. B.; *Character and Environment in the Novels of Thomas Hardy.* Witherby, London, 1925.

HARDY, FLORENCE EMILY; *The Early Life of Thomas Hardy, 1840-1891.* N. Y., 1928.

HARDY, FLORENCE EMILY; *The Later Years of Thomas Hardy, 1892-1928.* London, 1930.

HARPER, CHAS. G.; *The Hardy Country: Literary Landmarks of the Wessex Novels.* London, 1904.

HEDGECOCK, F. A.; *Thomas Hardy, Penseur et Artiste.* Hachette, Paris, 1911.

HIND, C. L.; *Authors and I.* 1921.

HOLLIDAY, CARL; *English Fiction from the Fifth to the Twentieth Century.* N. Y., 1912.

HOPKINS, R. T.; *Thomas Hardy's Dorcet.* N. Y., 1922.

HOWELLS, WM. DEAN; *Heroines of Fiction.* V. 2 N. Y., 1901.

JAMES, WILLIAM; *Varieties of Religious Experience* (Lecture) N. Y., 1902.

JOHNSON, LIONEL; *The Art of Thomas Hardy,* including Bibliography of Hardy's Works by John Lane. London 1894.

KILMER, JOYCE; *Introduction to Modern Literary Edition of The Mayor of Caster-bridge*, N. Y., 1917.

KORTEN, HERTHA; *Thomas Hardy's Napoleondichtung: The Dynasts: Ihre Abhangkeit von Schopenhauer: Ihr Einfluss auf Gerhart Hauptmann.* Bonn 1919.

LANE, JOHN; "Bibliography of First Editions of Thomas Hardy," in Lionel Johnson's *Art of Thomas Hardy.* London, 1894.

LAPARRA, MADAME F.; "*Jude L'Obscur, traduction intergrale.*" Stock, Paris.

LEBRAUD, VALÉRY; *Ce Vice Impuni, La Lecture.* Chap. VIII, "Thomas Hardy, Dramaturge". Paris, 1925.

LASSELIN, GEORGE; *Le Couple Humain dans L'Oeuvre de Thomas Hardy.* Paris, 1928.

LEA, HERMANN; *A Handbook of the Wessex Country of Mr. Hardy's Novels and Poems.* London, 1906.

LEA, HERMANN; *Thomas Hardy's Wessex.* London, 1913.

LIRON, A.; *La Femme dans le Roman de Hardy*, 1919.

LYND, ROBERT; *Old and New Masters*, Chap. XXVII. London, 1919.

MACDONNELL, ANNIE; *Thomas Hardy.* N. Y., 1895.

McDOWALL, ARTHUR S.; *Thomas Hardy.* London, 1931.

MACTAGGART, J. T. L.; *Some Dogmas of Religion.* London, 1906.

MAGNUS, LAURIE; *English Literature in the Nineteenth Century.* London, 1909.

MAIS, S. P. B.; *From Shakespeare to O'Henry.* Chapter XI, "The Poetry of Thomas Hardy." N. Y., 1923.

MARGUERITTE, EVA PAUL; "*La Bien-Aimée*, roman traduit de l'anglais." Plon, Paris, 1909.

MARGUERITTE, EVA PAUL; "*Deux Yeux Bleus*, roman traduit de l'anglais." Plon, Paris, 1913.

MARGUERITTE, EVA PAUL; "Le Retour au Pays Natal, roman traduit de l'anglais." Flammarion, Paris, 1923.

MARGUERITTE, EVA PAUL; "*Sous La Verte Feuillée*, roman traduit de l'anglais." Flammarion, Paris, 1924.

MAXWELL, DONALD; *The Landscape of Thomas Hardy.* London, 1928.

MONTFORT, EUGENE; *Réflections à propos de Thomas Hardy*, "Les Marges", 1903-08.

MORDELL, ALBERT; *Notorious Literary Attacks* (Reprints Lang's attack on *Tess*). N. Y., 1926.

MURRAY, D. C.; *My Contemporaries in Fiction.* London, 1897.

MURRY, J. MIDDLETON; *Aspects of Literature.* London, 1920.

NEWTON, A. E.; *Thomas Hardy, Novelist or Poet?* Phila., 1929.

OLIVERO, FEDERICO; *Un Introduzione a Thomas Hardy.* (Traduzione di A. Milcare Ramello.) 1931-

PHELPS, WILLIAM L.; *Essays on Modern Novelists.* 1910.

PHELPS, WILLIAM L.; *The Advance of the English Novel.* N. Y., 1916.

POWYS, J. C.; *Visions and Revisions.* 1915.

POWYS, LLEWELYN; *Thirteen Worthies.* N. Y., 1923.

PURDY, R. L.; *Thomas Hardy, O. M., 1840-1928.* Catalogue of a Memorial Exhibition of First Editions, Autographed Letters and MSS. Yale University Library, 1928.

QUILLER-COUCH, A. T.; *Adventures in Criticism.* London, 1896

QUILLER-COUCH, A. T.; "The Poetry of Thomas Hardy", *Studies in Literature.* Cambridge University Press, 1923.

ROLLAND, MLLE.; *"Tess d'Urbervilles,* roman traduit de l'anglais." Hatchette, Paris, 1901 Nouvelle èdit: La Sirène, 1914.

ROLLI, AUGUSTUS; *Critiques.* "The Heart of the Wessex Novels." London, 1927.

RAYMOND, E. T.; *Portraits of the Nineties,* pp. 211-220. N. Y., 1921.

ROZ, FIRMIN; *Le Roman Anglais Contemporain.* Paris, 1912.

SACHS, J. J.; *The Harrowing Contingencies of Human Experience.* "Some Reflections on Hardy." Quarto Club Papers, 1927-28. N. Y., 1929.

SALBERG, GERDA; *Thomas Hardy's Frauen im Lichte seiner Weltanschauung.* Zürich, 1927.

SAXELBY, F. O.; *A Thomas Hardy Dictionary.* London, 1911.

SCHOLL, ANNA M.; *Thomas Hardy.* Warner Library, v. 12, p. 6931, 1917.

SCOTT, J. R. A.; *Modernism and Romance,* pp. 57-68. 1908.

SELBY, T. G.; *The Theology of Modern Fiction.* London, 1896.

SHAFER, ROBERT; *Christianity and Naturalism.* Yale Press, 1926.

SHERMAN, STUART P.; *Contemporary Literature.* 1917.

SHERREN, WILKINSON; *The Wessex of Romance.* London, 1902.

SIME, G.; *Thomas Hardy of the Wessex Novels.* Carrier, Montreal, 1928.

SQUIRE, J. C.; *Essays on Poetry.* London, 1923.

SWANN, GEORGE R.; *Philosophical Parallelisms in Six English Novelists.* U. of Penna. Thesis, Phila., 1929.

SYMONDS ARTHUR; *Figures of Several Centuries,* 1916.

Bibliography

TAUFKIRCH, R.; *Die Romankunst von Thomas Hardy.* Marburg, 1912.

VALOKIS, A. P. D.; *Lachrymae Rerum: The Moira of Aeschylus and the Immanent Will of Thomas Hardy.* 1928.

VAN DOREN, CARL AND MARK; *American and British Literature Since 1890.* N. Y., 1925.

VILLARD, LÉONIE, *La Femme Anglaise au XIXe Siecle* (et Son Evolution D'apres le Roman Anglais Contemporain) Henri Didier, Paris, 1920.

VINCENT, LEON H.; *The Bibliotaph and Other Papers*, pp. 80-112. 1898.

VINCIGUERIA, MARIO; *Romantici e decedenti inglesi.* 1926.

WEBB, A. P.; *A Bibliography of the Works of Thomas Hardy.* London, 1916.

WEYGANDT, CORNELIUS; *A Century of the English Novel.* N. Y., 1925.

WHITFIELD, A. S.; *Thomas Hardy, the Artist, the Man and the Disciple of Destiny.* London, 1921.

WILLIAMS, HAROLD; *Two Centuries of the English Novel*, Chapter XVI, "Hardy." London, 1911.

WILLIAMS, RANDALL; *The Wessex Novels of Thomas Hardy.* London, 1924.

WILSON, S. L.; *The Theology of Modern Literature*, Chapter VIII; "The Theology of Thomas Hardy." Edinburgh, 1899.

WINDLE, B. C. A.; *The Wessex of Thomas Hardy*, London, 1902.

ZACHRISSON, R. E.; *Thomas Hardy As Man, Writer, and Philosopher* with a Swedish Hardy Bibliography. Stockholm, 1928.

PART II

MAGAZINE ARTICLES, REVIEWS, CRITICISMS, AND OBITUARIES

ABERCROMBIE, LASCELLES; "Review of the Famous Tragedy of the Queen of Cornwall at Tintagel in Lyonesse." *Nation-Athenaeum*, v. XXXIV, p. 491 London, Dec. 29, 1923.

ABERNATHY, J. W.; "The Invasion of Realism." *Education*, v. 21 pp. 469-474.

ADCOCK, A. ST. JOHN; "Gods of Modern Grub Street." *Canadian Magazine*, v. 61, 33-37, May, 1923.

ADCOCK, A. ST. JOHN; "Thomas Hardy." *The Bookman*, v. 73, pp. 263-266, London, 1928.

ALDINGTON, RICHARD; "Conrad and Hardy." *New York Evening Post Literature Review.* p. 8, Sept. 6, 1924.

ALEXANDER, GRACE; "Thomas Hardy, Wizard of Essex." *New Republic*, v. 23, pp. 335-336, Aug. 18, 1920.

ALEXANDER, HOOPER; "Hardy's Plagiarism." *New Republic*, v. 54, p. 71, Feb. 29, 1928.

ARCHER, WILLIAM; "Real Conversations." *Critic*, v. 38, pp. 309-318, April, 1901.

ARMSTRONG, MARTIN; "Review of the Famous Tragedy of the Queen of Cornwall." *Spectator*, v. 131, p. 904, London, Dec. 8, 1923.

ARONSTEIN, PHIL; In "Germanisch-romanische Monatsschrift." 1914.

AYNARD, JOSEPH; *Revue de Paris*, v. 4, 1903.

AYNARD, JOSEPH; "Les Dernières Années de Thomas Hardy; à propos du livre de F. E. Hardy" *Journal des Débats*, Oct. 3, 1930.

AYSCOUGH, JOHN; "Last Giants." *Catholic World*, v. 100, pp. 776-783, March, 1915.

BAGSHAW, WM.; "Thomas Hardy." *Manchester Quarterly*, pp. 99-114, April, 1923.

BAILEY, JOHN; "Thomas Hardy, on the Publication of A Changed Man." *The Bookman*, London, v. 45, pp. 143-145; Dec., 1913.

BARRIE, J. M.; "Thomas Hardy: the Historian of Wessex." *Contemporary Review*, v. 56, pp. 57-66; July, 1889.

BATES, EARNEST S.; "The Optimism of Thomas Hardy." *International Journal of Ethics*, v. 15, pp. 469-485; July, 1905.

BAUËR, GÉRARD; "Le Coeur et les Centres de Thomas Hardy." *Echo de Paris*, Jan 19, 1928.

BEACH, JOSEPH W.; "Hardy's Romantic Adventures of a Milkmaid." *Nation*, v. 94, pp. 82-83; Jan. 25, 1912.

BEACH, JOSEPH W.; "Hardy's 'What the Shepherd Saw' " *Nation*, v. 94, p. 107, Feb., 1912.

BEACH, JOSEPH W.; "Bowdlerized Versions of Hardy." *P. M. L. A.*, v. 36, pp. 632-643, Dec., 1921.

BEERHOLM, MAX; "Thomas Hardy as Panoramist." *Living Age*, v. 240, pp. 507-510, Feb. 20, 1904.

BENNETT, ARNOLD; "The True Greatness of Thomas Hardy." *Evening Standard*, Jan. 12, 1928.

BENSON, A. C.; "Realism in Fiction." *North American*, v. 195, pp. 820-832.

BENSUSAN, S. L.; "Thomas Hardy", *Quarterly Review*, v. 253, pp. 313-329, Oct. 1929.

BICKLEY, FRANCIS; "Hardy's Poems", *The Bookman*, v. 54, pp. 12-13; London, April, 1918.

BINYON, LAWRENCE; "The Art of Thomas Hardy." (A review of "Satires of Circumstance") *The Bookman*, v. 47, pp. 143-144; Feb., 1915.

BLANCHE, J. E.; "Souvenirs de Thomas Hardy", *Nouvelles Litteraires;* Jan. 21, 1928.

BOURGET, PAUL; "Limits of Realism in Fiction." *Living Age*, v. 196, p. 737.

BOYD, ERNEST; "A New Way with Old Masterpieces", *Harpers*, v. 151, pp. 234-245, July, 1925.

BRASH, W. B.; "Thomas Hardy" *The London Quarterly Review*, v. 149, 5th series, v. 35; April, 1928.

BRASH, W. B.; "More About Thomas Hardy" (Review of Florence Emily Hardy's *Later Years of Thomas Hardy*) *The London Quarterly Review*, Oct., 1930.

BRONNER, MILTON; "The Art of Lionel Johnson," *Bookman*, v. 36, pp. 183-185, Oct., 1912.

BROWN, IVOR; "Reviews of the Queen of Cornwall" *Saturday Review*, v. 136, pp. 613-614; London.

BROWN, VINCENT; "Thomas Hardy: On Enthusiasm" *The Academy*, v. 58, p. 208; Mar. 10, 1900.

BURDETT, O.; "Hardy Biography" *London Mercury*, v. 22, pp. 250-257; June 1930.

Bush, Donald; "The Varied Hues of Pessimism" *Dalhousie Review*, v. 9, pp. 271-281; Oct., 1929.

Busse, Kurt; "Thomas Hardy and Wir." *Preussische Jarhesbucher*, 1928.

Butler, A. J.; "Mr. Hardy as a Decadent." *National Review*, v. 27, pp. 384-390; May, 1896.

Castellan, Maurice; "The Dynasts." *Revue Germanique*, pp. 354.

Chang, Hain-Hai; "A Chinese Estimate of Hardy's Poetry." *The Hibbert Journal*, v. 27, pp. 78-92; Oct., 1928.

Chevalley, Abel; *Revue de Paris*, Feb., 1928.

Chew, S. C.; "Homage to Thomas Hardy." *The New Republic*, v. 23, pp. 22-26; June, 1920.

Chew, S. C.; "Review of the Queen of Cornwall". *The New Republic*, v. 38, pp. 23-24; Feb. 27, 1924.

Child, Harold; "Thomas Hardy" (An appreciation on his eightieth birthday.) *The Bookman*, v. 58, pp. 101-103; June, 1920, London.

Christofaro, C.; "Tommaso Hardy," in *Rassegra Nazionale*, Anno. 50, ser. 3, v. 1, 1928.

Church, Richard; "Thomas Hardy." *Spectator*, v. 140, pp. 71-72; Jan., 1928.

Clark, G. H.; "Thomas Hardy and His Biography." *Queen's Quarterly*, v. 38, pp. 280-305; April, 1928.

Collins, Vere H.; "Talks with Thomas Hardy." *The Bookman*, v. 67, pp. 1-6; March, 1928.

Colum, Padraic; "Robert Bridges and Thomas Hardy." *The New Republic*, v. 12, pp. 47-49; Aug., 11, 1917.

Columbine, W. B.; "The Poems of Thomas Hardy." *Westminister Review*, v. 152, pp. 180-184; Aug., 1899.

Colvin, Ian; "Thomas Hardy: An Elegy" (Poem) *Living Age*, v. 334, p. 337; Feb. 15, 1928.

Conacher, W. M.; "Jude the Obscure—A Study." *Queen's Quarterly*, v. 35, pp. 329-340; Autum, 1928.

Courtney, W. L.; "Mr. Thomas Hardy and Aeschylus." *Fortnightly*, v. 107, pp. 464-477; March, 1917 and v. 107, pp. 629-640; April, 1917.

Cross, W.; "Thomas Hardy and His Readers". *Yale Review*, v. 20, pp. 175-177; Sept., 1930.

Danielson, Henry; "Bibliographies of Modern Authors; no. 12, Thomas Hardy." *The Bookman's Journal and Print Collector*, v. 1, pp. 454, 469, 489; April 9, 16, 23, 1920.

DARTON, F. J. H.; "Thomas Hardy's Birthplace." *Living Age*, v. 324, pp. 303-305; Feb., 1925.

DAVIS, F. H.; "The Hardy Players." *Drama*, v. 13, pp. 359-360; Aug., 1923.

DAVRAY, HENRI D.; "Thomas Hardy et Son Temps." *Mercure de France*, v. 202, pp. 5-19; Feb., 1928.

DAUDET, LÉON; *"L'Action Francaise;* Jan 16, 1928.

DE CASSERAS, BENJAMIN; "Thomas Hardy's Women." *The Bookman*, v. 16, pp. 131-133; Oct., 1902.

DE LA MARE, WALTER; *"The Dynasts*, A Review of v. III." *The Bookman*, v. 34, pp. 110-112; June, 1908, London.

DENIS, MADAME MAURICE; "Poems de Thomas Hardy, Traduis." *Revue Hebdomadaire.* "Deux des Petites Ironies De La Vie," en feuilleton dans le *Journal des Debats.* 1901

DICKENSON, THOMAS H.; "Thomas Hardy's *The Dynasts*", *North American Review*, v. 195, pp. 526-542; April, 1912.

DOLMAN, FREDERICK; "An Evening with Thomas Hardy." *The Young Man;* March, 1894.

DOUGLAS, SIR GEORGE; "Wessex Novels." *The Bookman*, v. 17, pp. 110-112; Jan., 1900, London.

DOUGLAS, SIR GEORGE; "Thomas Hardy: Some Recollections and Reflections." *The Hibbert Journal*, v. 26, pp. 385-398; April, 1928.

DURRANT, W. S.; "The Disciple of Destiny." *Living Age*, v. 262, pp. 221-227; July, 1924.

ELLIOTT, G. R.; "Hardy's Poetry and the Ghostly Moving Picture." *The South Atlantic Quarterly*, v. 27, pp. 280-291; July, 1928.

ELLIOTT, G. R.; "Spectral Etching in the Poetry of Thomas Hardy." *P. M. L. A.*, v. 43, pp. 1183-1195; Dec., 1928.

ELLIS, S. M.; "Thomas Hardy: Some Personal Recollections." *Fortnightly*, v. 129, pp. 393-406; March, 1928.

EWART, WILFRED; "Thomas Hardy and Our Own Times." *Nineteenth Century*, v. 90, pp. 427-437; Sept., 1921.

FAIRLEY, BARKER; "Notes on the Form of *The Dynasts*." *P. M. L. A.*, v. 34, pp. 401-415; Sept., 1919.

FAIRLEY, BARKER; "Thomas Hardy's Lyrical Poems." *Canadian Bookman.* v. 2, pp. 18-22; July, 1920.

FLETCHER, J. G.; "Thomas Hardy" (Poem) *The Bookman*, v. 68, p. 621; Feb., 1929.

FLETCHER, J. G.; "Thomas Hardy's Poetry." *Poetry*, v. 16, pp. 43-49; April, 1920.

FLETCHER, J. G.; "The Spirit of Thomas Hardy." *Yale Review*, n. s., v. 13, pp. 322-333; Jan., 1924.

FLETCHER, J. G.; "The Black Rock: to Thomas Hardy." (Poem) *The Yale Review*, v. 17, n. s., pp. 447-451; April, 1928.

FLOWER, NEWMAN; "In His Wessex Home." *Sunday Times*, London, Jan. 15, 1928.

FOLLET, HELEN AND WILSON; "The Historian of Wessex." *Atlantic Monthly*, v. 120, pp. 356-366; Sept., 1917.

FORSYTH, P. T.; "The Pessimism of Mr. Thomas Hardy." (From the *London Quarterly Review*.) *The Living Age*, v. 275, pp. 458-473; Nov., 1912.

FOURNIER-PAGOIRE, JEANNE; "Poems of Thomas Hardy, traduction." *Les Marges*, 1925.

FRANKS, ARTHUR; "Sous La Verte Feuillée, traduit de l'anglais." Feuilleton de *Paris-Journal;* Juillet et Août, 1910.

FREEMAN, JOHN; "Poetry, Prophecy and the War." *Nineteenth Century*, v. 77, pp. 631-647; March, 1915.

FREEMAN, JOHN; "The Poetry of Thomas Hardy." *The Bookman*, v. 57, pp. 139-141; Jan., 1920.

FREEMAN, JOHN; "Thomas Hardy." *London Mercury*, v. 17, pp. 532-544; March, 1928.

FRIEDLAENDER, V. H.; "Early Spring and Hardy." (Poem) *Fortnightly*, v. 131, pp. 265; Feb., 1929.

FRYE, PROSSER H.; "Nature and Thomas Hardy." *The Independent*, v. 54, pp. 1657-1659; July, 1902.

FUESS, C. M.; "Thomas Hardy Among the Immortals." *Boston Transcript;* Jan. 28, 1928.

FURNISS, HARRY; "Thomas Hardy, O. M." *Strand Magazine*, v. 66, pp. 252-256; Sept., 1923.

GARRET, LINDSAY S.; "The Essence of Hardyism." *Monthly Review*, v. 27, iii, 59; June, 1907.

GARSTANG, A. H.; "The Humour of Thomas Hardy." *Fortnightly*, v. 129, pp. 205-209; Feb., 1928.

GIBSON, WILFRED; "Hardy's Short Stories." *The Bookman*, v. 74, pp. 148-149; June, 1928.

GIBSON, WILFRED; "Hardy's Last Poems." *The Bookman*, v. 75, pp. 107-108; Nov., 1928.

GIGLI, LORENZO; "Thomas Hardy." *Nuova Antologia;* Jan. 16, 1928.

GILBERT, ARIADNE; "In Thomas Hardy's World." *St. Nicholas*, v. 55, pp. 357-358; March, 1928.

GILLET, LOUIS; "Thomas Hardy." *Revue des Deux Mondes;* Feb. 1, 1928.

GORMAN, H. S.; "Poems and Lyrics" (A Review of Hardy's *Late Lyrics and Earlier)_ Outlook*, v. 133, pp. 35-36; Jan. 3, 1923.

GOSSE, EDMUND; "Mr. Hardy's Lyrical Poems." *Edinburgh Review*, v. 227, pp. 272-293; April, 1918.

GOSSE, EDMUND; "The Historic Place of Mr. Meredith and Mr. Hardy." *International Monthly*, v. 4, pp. 299-323; Sept., 1901.

GOSSE, EDMUND; "Thomas Hardy." *The Speaker*, Sept. 13, 1890.

GRAVES, ROBERT; "Mr. Hardy and the Pleated Skirt" *Nation*, London, v. 33, pp. 451-452; July, 1933.

GREENWOOD, FREDERICK; "The Germs of Thomas Hardy." *Illustrated London News;* Oct. 1, 1892.

GRENZOW, D.; "Last of the Victorians." *World Review*, v. 5, p. 261; Jan., 1928.

GREY, ROWLAND; "Certain Women of Thomas Hardy." Fortnightly, v. 118, pp. 677-691; Oct., 1922.

GREY, ROWLAND; "The 'Jeune Premier' and Thomas Hardy." *Bookman*, v. 69, pp. 151-155; Dec., 1925.

GREY, ROWLAND; "Women in the Poetry of Thomas Hardy." *Fortnightly*, v. 125, pp. 34-47, Jan., 1926.

HANNIGAN, D. F.; "Mr. Thomas Hardy's Latest Novel." *Westminster Review*, v. 145, pp. 136-139; Feb., 1896.

HANNIGAN, D. F.; "The Latest Development of English Fiction." *Westminster Review*, v. 138, pp. 655-659; Dec., 1892.

HARPER, G. M.; "Hardy, Hudson, Hausman." *Scribner's*, v. 78, pp. 151-157; Aug., 1925.

HEATH, FREDERICK; "A Note on Thomas Hardy." *Bermondsey Book*, v. 5, pp. 59-63; March-May, 1928.

HEATH, FREDERICK; "A Stranger at Max Gate." *Literary Digest*, v. 87, p. 34; June, 1928.

HEDEN, E.; "Thomas Hardy." *Litteraturkritik*, I, pp. 22-37; 1927.

HELLSTROM, G.; "Thomas Hardy och ododligheten." *Dagens Nijheter;* Feb. 2, 1928.

HENDERSON, SIR ARCHIBALD; "Thomas Hardy in a New Role—The Story of Tristram and Yseult Retold"; *Forum*, v. 71 pp. 783-790; June 1924.

HENNEMAN, J. B.; "The Dramatic Novel—George Meredith and Thomas Hardy." *The Reader*, v. 8, pp. 680-685; Nov., 1908.

HIND, C. L.; "Two Poets: Thomas Hardy and Flecker." *Outlook*, v. 139, pp. 397; Feb., 1925.

HOLLAND, CLIVE; "Thomas Hardy, Novelist and Poet, The Man, His Country and His Books." *Review of Reviews*, v. 69, pp. 497-507; May, 1922, London.

HOLLAND, CLIVE; "A Painter of Thomas Hardy's Wessex; the work of Frederick Whitehead." *The Studio;* July, 1924.

HOLLAND, CLIVE; "A Pilgrimage to Wessex." *Critic*, v. 39, pp. 136-141; Aug., 1901.

HOLLAND, CLIVE; "Thomas Hardy's Country." *Bookman*, v. 9, pp. 328-340; 519-527; June, August, 1899.

HOLLAND, CLIVE; "Thomas Hardy As I Knew Him." *The Landmark*, v. 10, pp. 75-77; Feb., 1928.

HOLLAND, CLIVE; "Thomas Hardy and Wessex." *The Bookman*, v. 73, pp. 267-270; Feb., 1928.

HONE, J. M.; "The Poetry of Mr. Hardy." *London Mercury*, v. 5, pp. 396-405; Feb., 1922.

HONE, J. M.; "The Poetry of Thomas Hardy." *Living Age*, v. 313, pp. 52-57; April, 1922.

HOPKINS, F. M.; "The Field of Old Rare Books and Weekly Book Exchange." "A Check-List of the Work of Thomas Hardy." *The Publishers' Weekly*, v. 113, pp. 292-294; Jan., 1928.

HOWELLS, W. D.; "Review of *Poems of the Past and Present*." *North American Review*, v. 174, pp. 140-141; Jan., 1928.

JALOUX, EDMOND; "*Candide*, Jan. 19, 1928.

JOHNSON, LIONEL; "Academy Portraits—Thomas Hardy." *Academy*, v. 55, p. 251; Nov., 1898.

KENDALL, MAY; "Pessimism and Thomas Hardy's Poems." *London Quarterly*, v. 91, pp. 223-234.

KING, GEORGE; "Thomas Hardy: Novelist and Poet." *Cornhill*, n. s., v. 64, pp. 298-291; March, 1928.

KING, MARIANNE; "Temperamental Pessimism in Thomas Hardy." *Pacific Review*, v. 1, pp. 530-542; March, 1921.

KING, R. W.; "The Lyrical Poems of Thomas Hardy." *London Mercury*, v. 15, pp. 157-170; Dec., 1926.

KNICKERBOCKER, FRANCIS W.; "The Victorianness of Thomas Hardy." *Sewanee Review*, v. 36, pp. 310-325; July, 1928.

KNOWLES, DAVID; "The Thought and Art of Thomas Hardy." *Dublin Review*, v. 183, pp. 208-218; Oct., 1927.

LANG, ANDREW; "At the Sign of the Ship." *Longman's Magazine*, v. 21, pp. 100-106; Nov., 1892.

LAWRENCE, N. S.; "The Turberville of Tess." *Chamber's Journal*, series 7, v. 18, pp. 628-630; Sept., 1928.

LEE, VERNON; "The Handling of Words: Thomas Hardy." *The English Review*, v. 9, pp. 231-241; Sept., 1911.

LEFÉVRE, FRÉDÉRICK; "An Hour With Thomas Hardy." *Living Age*, v. 325, pp. 98-103; April, 1925.

LE GALLIENNE, RICHARD; "Wanderings in Bookland." *The Idler*, v. 9, pp. 114-115; Feb., 1896.

LEVY, O.; "Thomas Hardy and Frederick Nietzsche." *Outlook*, v. 61, pp. 217-218; Feb., 1928.

LOGAN, A. M.; "Review of Johnson's *Art of Thomas Hardy*." *The Nation*, v. 60, pp. 225-226; March, 1895.

LOWES, JOHN L.; "Two Readings of Earth." *Yale Review*, n. s., v. 15, pp. 515-539; April, 1926.

MACAFEE, HELEN; "Review of *The Queen of Cornwall*." *Yale Review*, n. s. ,v. 14, pp. 385; Jan., 1925.

MACARTHUR, JAMES ; "Books and Bookmen." *Harper's Weekly*, v. 49, p. 1486; Oct., 1905.

MACCARTHY, DESMOND; "Thomas Hardy" (A review of the *Early Life of Thomas Hardy*, by Florence E. Hardy.) *Saturday Review*, v. 5, pp. 421-422; Dec., 1928.

MACFALL, HALDANE; "Thomas Hardy" *Canadian Magazine*, v. 23, pp. 105-108; 1904.

MACY, JOHN; "Two-fold Genius of Thomas Hardy." *Bookman*, v. 67, pp. 134-139; April, 1928.

MAINSARD, JOSEPH; "*Etudes*, Tome, 191, p. 439; 1927.

MARBLE, ANNIE R.; "Hardy Again." *Saturday Review*, v. 2, p. 296; May, 1926.

MARTIN, DOROTHY; "Thomas Hardy's Lyrics." *Freeman*, v. 8, pp. 490-492, 515-516; Jan., Feb., 1924.

MARTIN, G. C.; "Thomas Hardy and the English Bible." *Bookman*, London, v. 74, pp. 24-26; April, 1928.

MAYOUX, J. J.; "L'Amour dans les Romans de Hardy." *Revue Anglo-Américaine*;, Feb., 1928.

MAYOUX, J. J.; "La Fatalité intérieure dans les Romans de Hardy." *Revue Anglo-Americaine;* Jan., Feb., 1927.

MAYNARD, THEODORE; "The Poetry of Thomas Hardy." *Catholic World*, v. 123, pp. 46-54; April, 1926.

McGRATH, FERGAL; "The Pessimism of Thomas Hardy." *Studies (An Irish Quarterly Review.)* v. 17, pp. 29-38; March, 1928.

McNUTT, R. D.; "A Visit to Mr. Thomas Hardy." *Delhousie Review*, v. 6, pp. 51-55; April, 1926.

MEIBERGEN, C. R.; "The Woodlanders." *Englische Studien*, v. 51, pp. 226-247; Oct., 1917.

MEYERFELD, MAX; "The Dynasts." *Literarisches Echo;* 1904-1905.

MILNE, JAMES; "Mr. Hardy's Birthday." *Book Monthly*, v. 14, pp. 472-474; June, 1919.

MINTO, WM.; "The Work of Thomas Hardy." *Bookman*, Dec., 1891.

MONROE, HARRIET; "Thomas Hardy." *Poetry*, v. 31, pp. 326-332; March, 1928.

MORLEY, CHRISTOPHER; "Touch Wood." *Saturday Review*, v. 4, p. 533; Jan., 1928.

MORRIS, LLOYD; "Hardy, the Great Pagan." *The Open Court*, v. 42, pp. 382-384; June, 1928.

MOSS, MARY; "The Novels of Thomas Hardy." *Atlantic Monthly*, v. 98, pp. 354-367; Sept., 1906.

MUIR, EDWIN; "The Novels of Thomas Hardy." *New York Evening Post Literary Review*, pp. 801-802; June 7, 1924.

MURRAY, DAVID C.; "My Contemporaries in Fiction." *Canadian Magazine*, v. 9, pp. 38-41; May, 1897.

MURRY, J. MIDDLETON; "The Supremacy of Thomas Hardy." *The New Adelphi*, v. 1, pp. 219-224; March, 1928.

NAIRNE, A.; "The Poetry of Thomas Hardy." *"Living Age*, v. 302, pp. 175-178; July, 1919.

NEEL, P. H.; "Le Maire de Casterbridge, roman traduit de l'anglais." *Nouvelle Revue* Francaise; Paris, 1922.

NEWBOLT, HENRY; "A New Departure in English Poetry." *Quarterly Review*, pp. 134; 1909.

NEWTON-ROBIŅSON, JANETTA; "A Study of Mr. Thomas Hardy." *Westminster Review*, v. 137, pp. 153-164; Feb., 1892.

NOYES, ALFRED; "The Poetry of Thomas Hardy." *North American Review*, v. 194, pp. 96-105; July, 1911.

NOYES, ALFRED; "To Thomas Hardy on His Eighty-third Birthday." *Literary Digest*, p. 34; July 14, 1923.

O'Connor, T. P.; "Thomas Hardy as I knew Him." From *Daily Telegraph*, Jan., 13, 1928. *Living Age*, v. 334, pp. 454-457; March, 1928.

Oliphant, M. O. W.; "The Anti-Marriage League." *Blackwood*, v. 159, pp. 135-149; Jan. 1896.

Olivero, F.; "The Poetry of Hardy." *The Poetry Review*, v. 20, pp. 1-22; Jan.-Feb., 1896.

O'Rourke, Rev. James; "The Orthodoxy of Thomas Hardy." *Irish Ecclesiastical Record*, v. 33, series 5, pp. 237-245; March, 1929.

Orr, Lyndon; "Thomas Hardy and Longstreet." *Bookman*, v. 22, pp. 635-636; Feb., 1906 Bookman, v. 23, pp. 121-126; April, 1906.

Overton, G.; "Do You Remember *Tess of the D'Urbervilles?*" *Mentor*, v. 17, p. 45; Sept., 1929.

Parker, W. M.; "Christmas With Thomas Hardy." *Fortnightly*, v. 122, pp. 804-816; Dec., 1924.

Parker, W. M.; "The Genius of Thomas Hardy." *The Nineteenth Century*, v. 88, pp. 63-71; July, 1920.

Parker, W. M.; "The Jubilee of *Far From the Madding Crowd*, 1874-1924." *Cornhill*, v. 56, pp. 119-126; Jan., 1924.

Parker, W. M.; "My Visit to Thomas Hardy: A Memorable Day at Max Gate." *Cornhill*, v. 66, pp. 278-291; March, 1928.

Phelps, W. L.; "As I Like it." *Scribners*, v. 85, pp. 221-423; Feb., 1929.

Phelps, W. L.; "The Novels of Thomas Hardy." *North American Review*, v. 190, pp. 502-514; Oct., 1909.

Phelps, W. L.; "Thomas Hardy." *Saturday Review*, v. 1, p. 808; June, 1905.

Phelps, W. L.; "William Lyon Phelps Lines Up Thomas Hardy." *The American Review of Reviews*, v. 73, p. 320; March, 1926.

Phelps, W. L.; "Thomas Hardy's Fifteen Novels." *Forum*, v. 79, pp. 436-447; March, 1928.

Phelps, W. L.; "A Thomas Hardy Memorial." *Saturday Review*, v. 4, p. 785; April, 1928.

Phillips, Charles; "The Hardy Optimists." *Catholic World*, v. 108, pp. 762-766; March, 1919.

Phillpotts, Eden; "To Thomas Hardy." (Poem) (From *The Atheneum*) *Living Age*, v. 306, p. 173; July, 1921.

Pollock, John; "The Dynasts." *Independent Review*, v. 4, pp. 149-155; Nov., 1904.

Powell, G. H.; "The Weird of Wessex." *Oxford and Cambridge Review*, no. 22, pp. 55-70; August, 1912.

Powys, J. C.; "Thomas Hardy and His Times." *Current History*, v. 27, pp. 829-831; March, 1928.

Powys, Llewelyn; "Glimpses of Thomas Hardy." *The Dial*, v. 72, pp. 286-290; March, 1922.

Preston, Harriet W.; "Thomas Hardy." *The Century*. v. 46, pp. 353-359; July, 1893.

Prilipp, B.; "Thomas Hardy's Napoleonsdrama." *Die Grenzboten*, 1907.

Puaux, René; Two articles. *Le Temps;* Jan. 13, 1928, Jan. 17, 1928.

Puccio, Guido; *Rassegna Italiana.* March 1928.

Quiller-Couch, Sir Arthur; "The Poetry of Thomas Hardy." *Studies in Literature*, Cambridge University Press, 1923.

Reilly, J. J.; "Bazin and Hardy: A Study in Comparison with Contrast." *Catholic World*, v. 114, pp. 629, 640; Feb., 1922.

Reilly, J. J.; "Short Stories of Thomas Hardy." *Catholic World*, v. 128, pp. 407-415; Jan., 1929.

Rendall, Vernon; "Thomas Hardy, O. M." *English Review*, v. 46, pp. 192-195; Feb., 1928.

Ridder-Barzin, Louise de; In Université de Bruxelles *Revue*, Année 33, p. 315, 1928.

Rolleston, T. W.; "Life and Death: Considerations on a Poem of Thomas Hardy." *The Hibbert Journal*, v. 18, pp. 275-288; Jan., 1920.

Rolli, Augustus; "The Heart of the Wessex Novels." *North American Review*, v. 217, pp. 688-697; May, 1923.

Romlinson, H. M.; "Hardy at Max Gate." *The Saturday Review of Literature;* Feb. 11, 1928.

Roz, Firmin; "*Jude L'Obscure*, roman traduit de l'anglais" Ollendorf, Paris; 1903.

Salviris, Jacob; "A Reading of the Wessex Novels." *Westminster Review*, v. 178, pp. 400-412; Oct., 1912.

Sapir, E.; "Realism in Prose Fiction." *Dial*, v. 63, pp. 583-593; July, 1892.

Sherren, Wilkinson; "Thomas Hardy, O. M., 86." *Review of Reviews*, (London) v. 73, pp. 555-556; June and July, 1926.

Shuster, George N.; "Thomas Hardy." *Catholic World*, v. 126, pp. 721-729; March, 1928.

Simon, Pure; "Mr. Shaw, Mr. Hardy, and the Nobel Prize." *Bookman*, v. 64, pp. 720-721; Feb., 1927.

Smith, R. M.; Philosophy in Thomas Hardy's Poetry." *North American Review*, v. 220, pp. 330-340; Dec., 1924.

SOLA PINTO, V. DE; "Thomas Hardy." *Wessex:* An Annual Record of the Movement for a University of Wessex, pp. 16-20; 1928.

SQUIRE, J. C.; "Tristram and the Mummers." (A Review of the *Queen of Cornwall*) *London Times Supplement;* Nov. 15, 1923.

SQUIRE, J. C.; "A Review of *The Queen of Cornwall.*" *London Mercury,* v. 9; Dec, 1923.

SQUIRE, J. C.; "A Review of *The Queen of Cornwall.*" *Saturday Review* (London) v. 136, pp. 704-705; Dec., 1923.

STANLEY, CARLETON; "Poetry of Thomas Hardy." *Nineteenth Century,* v. 108, pp. 266-280; August, 1930.

STEPHENS, JAMES; "An Essay in Cubes." *The English Review,* v. 17, pp. 83-94; April, 1914.

STEVENSON, R. L.; "Realism." *Critic,* v. 18, p. 129.

STEWART, AGNES; "The Dynasts: A Psychological Interpretation." *English Review,* v. 38, pp. 666-680; May, 1924.

STEWART, H. L.; "Thomas Hardy as an Artist of Character." *University Magazine,* v. 17, pp. 247-261; April, 1918.

STEWART, H. L.; "Thomas Hardy as a Teacher of His Age." *North American Review,* v. 208, pp. 584-596; Oct., 1918.

STOPES, M. C.; "To Thomas Hardy, O. M." (Poem) *Nation,* London, v. 46, p. 893; March, 1930.

STURMER, H. H.; "In Hardy's Wessex." *Living Age,* v. 227, Oct., 27, Nov. 10, Nov. 17, and Dec. 29, 1900.

SYMONS, ARTHUR; "A Note on the Genius of Thomas Hardy." *The Saturday Review,* v. 102, pp. 391; Sept., 1906.

SYMONS, ARTHUR; "Thomas Hardy." *The Dial,* v. 68, pp. 66-70; Jan., 1920.

THOMPSON, MAURICE; "Studies of Prominent Novelists." (No. 4 Thomas Hardy.) *Book News,* v. 6, pp. 223-224; Jan., 1888.

TOMLINSON, H. M.; "The England of Hardy." *New Republic,* v. 25, pp. 190-192; Jan., 1921.

TOMLINSON, H. M.; "Hardy at Max Gate." *Saturday Review of Literature,* v. 4, pp. 585-587; Feb., 1928.

TRENT, W. P.; "The Dynasts." *Forum,* v. 38, p. 86; July, 1906.

TRENT, W. P.; "Mr. Thomas Hardy." *The Citizen,* v. 1, pp. 284-286; Feb., 1928.

TRUEBLOOD, CHARLES K.; "Tragedian of Sentence." *Dial,* v. 86, pp. 150-154.

TRUMAN, JOSEPH; "Tess and Angel Clare." (Poem) *Bookman,* London, v. 2, p. 11; April, 1892.

TURNBULL, M. M.; "Two Delineators of Wessex." *Gentleman's Magazine*, v. 71, n. s. pp. 469-479; Nov., 1903.

TYRELL, R. Y.; "Jude the Obscure." *Fortnightly*, v. 65, pp. 857-864; June 1, 1896.

URBAN, SYLVANUS; "A Notice of *Tess*." *Gentleman's Magazine*, v. 273, n. s. 49, p. 321; Sept., 1892.

UTTER, R. P.; "The Work of Thomas Hardy." *The Sewanee Review*, v. 35, pp. 129-138; April, 1917.

VALAKIS, APOLLO P. D.; "The Moira of Aeschylus and the Immanent Will of Thomas Hardy." *Classical Journal*, v. 21, pp. 431-442; March, 1926.

VAN DOREN, CARL; "Anatole France and Thomas Hardy." *Century*, v. 87, pp. 418-423; Jan., 1925.

VAN DOREN, CARL; "Thomas Hardy." *Outlook*, v. 148, p. 154; Jan, 1928.

VAN DOREN, MARK; "Thomas Hardy, Poet." *Nation*, v. 126, pp. 151-152; Feb., 1928.

WAGENKNECHT, EDWARD; "Review of Florence Emily Hardy's *Later Years of Thomas Hardy*." *Virginia Quarterly Review*, v. 6, pp. 621-624; October, 1930.

WATSON, WILLIAM; "Review of *Tess*." *Academy*, v. 41, pp. 125-126; Feb., 1892.

WEST, REBECCA; "Interpretation of Their Age." *Saturday Review*, v. 1, pp. 41-42; Aug., 1924.

WHIBLEY, CHARLES; "Thomas Hardy." *Blackwood's*, v. 193, pp. 823-831; June, 1913.

WHITE, J. W.; "In Thomas Hardy's Country." *Nation*, v. 55, pp. 184-185; 200-202; Sept., 1892.

WHITMORE, CHARLES E.; "Mr. Hardy's *Dynasts* as Tragic Drama." *Modern Language Notes*, v. 39, pp. 455-460; Dec., 1924.

WILLCOX, LOUISE C.; "Thomas Hardy." *The North American Review*, v. 201, pp. 423-429; March, 1915.

WILLIAMS, HAROLD; "The Wessex Novels of Thomas Hardy." *North American Review*, v. 199, pp. 120-134; Jan., 1914.

WOOD, WILLIAM; "More on Hardy." *Saturday Review*, v. 2, p. 666; March, 1926.

WOOLF, L.; "Thomas Hardy." *The Nation*, London, v. 42, pp. 597-598; Jan., 1928.

WOOLF, L.; "Half of Thomas Hardy." (Review of *Early Life of Thomas Hardy* by Florence Emily Hardy.) *Nation*, London, v. 44, pp. 289-291; Nov., 1928.

WORSTER, W.; "Thomas Hardy." *Bookman*, London, v. 74, pp. 220-221; July, 1928.

WRIGHT, EDWARD; "The Novels of Thomas Hardy." *Quarterly Review*, v. 199, pp. 499-523; April, 1904.

ZANGWILL, LOUIS; "In the World of Art and Letters." *Cosmopolitan*, v. 26, pp. 582-583; March, 1899.

ZACHRISSON, R. E.; *Ord och Bild*, pp. 277-280; 1919.

ZACHRISSON, R. E.; *Dagens Nyheter*, Nov. 9, 1920.

ZACHRISSON, R. E.; *Social-Demokraten*, Nov. 30, 1920.

ZACHRISSON, R. E.; *Edda*, pp. 57-98; 1923.

ZACHRISSON, R. E.; *Studiekamraten*, 1928.

PART III

ANONYMOUS MAGAZINE ARTICLES

THE ACADEMY—"Mr. Thomas Hardy's Novels." v. 21, pp. 120-121; Feb., 1882.

THE ACADEMY—"Mr. Hardy As a Poet." v. 56, pp. 43-44; Jan., 1899.

ATHENEUM—A Review of *"Poems of the Past and Present,"* Part One. pp. 6-7; Jan., 1902.

ATHENEUM—A Review of "Hardy's *Dynasts.*" v. 1, p. 123; Jan., 1904.

ATHENEUM—A Review of "Hardy's *Time's Laughingstocks.*" p. 34; Jan. 8, 1910.

THE BOOK BUYER—"Thomas Hardy." v. 9, pp. 151-153; May, 1892.

THE BOOKMAN—London. A Review of *"Tess."* v. 1, pp. 179-180; Feb., 1892.

THE BOOKMAN—"Thomas Hardy: An appreciation on the Occasion of His Seventieth Birthday." v. 38, pp. 122-123; June, 1910.

THE BOOKMAN—"Thomas Hardy's Wessex." Oct., 1891.

BRITISH QUARTERLY REVIEW—"Mr. Hardy's Novels." v. 73, pp. 342-360; April, 1881.

CHAMBER'S JOURNAL—"'Tis Sixty Years Since." v. 15, s. 7, pp. 1-5; Dec., 1924.

CHAMBER'S JOURNAL—A reprint of "How I Built Myself a House." March 18, 1865.

CHICAGO POST LITERARY REVIEW—"Thomas Hardy's First Editions." April 8, 1927.

CURRENT LITERATURE—"The Heroic Optimism of Thomas Hardy." v. 39, pp. 154-155; August, 1905.

CURRENT LITERATURE—"Thomas Hardy's Panoramic Drama." v. 40, pp. 522-523; May, 1906.

CURRENT LITERATURE—"Is Hardy Overestimated?" v. 43, pp. 290-292; Sept., 1907.

CURRENT LITERATURE—"Thomas Hardy's Latest Production—Magnum Opus or Monstrocity?" v. 44, pp. 659-662; June, 1908.

CURRENT OPINION—"Hardy's Attitude Toward Love." v. 56, pp. 47-48; Jan., 1914.

CURRENT OPINION—"Amateurs Who Surprised Professionals in a Great Epic Drama." v. 68, pp. 643-645; May, 1920.

CURRENT OPINION—"The Great Tragedian of Modern Letters." v. 69, pp. 236-238; Aug., 1920.

DAILY MAIL—"Literary Portraits," XII: Mr. Hardy." July 6, 1907.

THE DIAL—"Comments." (Obituary) v. 84, pp. 179-180; Feb., 1928.

DORSET NATURAL HISTORY AND ANTIQUARIAN CLUB—"Thomas Hardy." v. 49, pp. 25-39; May, 1927 to May, 1928.

EDINBURGH REVIEW—Review of *"The Dynasts"* April, 1908.

EDINBURGH REVIEW—"The Wessex Drama." A review of Hedgecock's *Thomas Hardy, Penseur et Artiste.* v. 215, pp. 93-112; Jan., 1912.

ENGLISH ILLUSTRATED MAGAZINE—"Thomas Hardy at Home." v. 47, pp. 276-280; June, 1912.

GOOD WORDS—"Letters to Living Authors: VII, Thomas Hardy." v. 43, pp. 673-678; 1902.

HARPERS WEEKLY—"Some Poets, Old and New." v. 46, p. 52; Jan., 1902.

JOURNAL des DÉBATS—"Obituary." v. 35, pp. 119-120; Jan., 1928.

LITERARY DIGEST—"Thomas Hardy. Last of the Victorians." v. 96, pp. 36-41; Feb., 1928.

LITERARY DIGEST—"Westminster Abbey Irony." v. 96, p. 29; Feb., 1928.

LITERARY DIGEST—"Barrie Reviews Hardy." v. 11, p. 22; Feb., 1929.

LITERARY DIGEST—"Did Hardy Sham?" v. 110, p. 16; Sept., 1931.

LIVING AGE—From *The Speaker.* "Hardyana." v. 250, pp. 189-191.

LIVING AGE—From *The Nation.* "The Pessimism of Thomas Hardy." v. 255, pp. 180-182; Oct., 1907.

LIVING AGE—From *The Academy.* "Thomas Hardy." v. 261, pp. 302-309; May, 1909.

LIVING AGE—From The Times. "Mr. Hardy's New Poems." A review of *Time's Laughingstocks.* v. 264, pp. 306-310; Jan., 1910.

LIVING AGE—"The English Novel and Mr. Hardy." v. 270, pp. 630-636; Sept., 1911.

LIVING AGE—From *The Times.* "The Poetry of Thomas Hardy." v. 296, pp. 202-207; Jan., 1918.

LIVING AGE—"The New Realism." v. 212, p. 564.

LIVING AGE—"A Young Poet and an Old One." v. 314, pp. 367-368; Aug., 1922.

LIVING AGE—"Thomas Hardy at Work." v. 318, pp. 428; Sept., 1923.

LIVING AGE—From *The London Times*, July 20. "The Prince and the Poet." v. 318, pp. 516-519; Sept., 1923.

LIVING AGE—"Why Thomas Hardy Did Not Get the Nobel Prize." v. 320, pp. 381-382; Feb., 1924.

LIVING AGE—"Thomas Hardy and the Nobel Prize." v. 321, p. 212; June, 1924.

LONDON MERCURY—"Thomas Hardy's Death." v. 17, pp. 337-340; Feb., 1928.

THE LONDON QUARTERLY REVIEW—"The Art of Thomas Hardy." A review of Lionel Johnsons' *The Art of Thomas Hardy.* v. 140, pp. 107-110; July, 1923.

LONDON TIMES LITERARY SUPPLEMENT—"*The Dynasts.* Jan. 15, 1904.

LONDON TIMES LITERARY SUPPLEMENT—From *Living Age.* "The Poetry of Thomas Hardy." pp. 603-604; Dec. 14, 1917.

LONDON TIMES LITERARY SUPPLEMENT—"*The Dynasts* at Oxford." pp. 113-114; Feb. 19, 1920.

MONTHLY REVIEW—"*The Dynasts.*" v. 14, No. 2, pp. 1-12; March, 1904.

THE NATION—"The Love of Good Writing." v. 94, pp. 608-609; June, 1912.

THE NATION—"Thomas Hardy, Poet." v. 121, p. 319.

THE NATION—(London) "The Epic of Tragic History." v. 26, pp. 668-669; Feb., 1920.

NEW REPUBLIC—"Thomas Hardy." v. 53, pp. 260-261; Jan., 1928.

NEW STATESMAN—"Thomas Hardy." v. 30, pp. 459-460; Jan., 1928.

OUR DAY—"*Jude the Obscure.*" (A review) v. 16, pp. 101-104; Feb., 1896.

THE OUTLOOK—"Thomas Hardy of Wessex." v. 125, p. 369; June, 1920.

THE OUTLOOK—(London) "Thomas Hardy." v. 61, pp. 74-75; Jan., 1928.

REVIEW OF REVIEWS—"Thomas Hardy." v. 77, pp. 319-320; March, 1928.

REVUE NOUVELLE—"Numero d'Hommage." Contributions by Middleton Murry, James Joyce, Eden Phillpots, Rene Boyslesve, Marcel Proust, Jean Schlumberger, Roman Fernandez, J. L. Vandoyer, G. D. Hanghest, Franz Hellens, Edmond Jaloux, Pierre d'Exideuil, and Charles DuBas. Feb., 1928.

SATURDAY REVIEW—"*Jude the Obscure.*" v. 82, pp. 153-154; Feb., 1896.

SATURDAY REVIEW—"The Poetry of Thomas Hardy." v. 128, pp. 459-460; Nov., 1919.

SATURDAY REVIEW—"Mr. Thomas Hardy." v. 145, pp. 30-31; Jan., 1928.

SATURDAY REVIEW OF LITERATURE—"He Carried On." v. 4, pp. 529-532; Jan., 1928.

SATURDAY REVIEW OF LITERATURE—"Burial of Thomas Hardy's Heart in the Country Churchyard at Stinsford." *London Times.* v. 4, p. 613; Feb. 18, 1928.

SEWANEE REVIEW—"The Novels of Thomas Hardy." v. 1, pp. 1-25; Nov., 1892.

Sewanee Review—"The Art of Thomas Hardy." A review of Johnson's book. v. 3, pp. 447-456; Aug., 1895.

The Spectator—"Mr. Hardy's *Tess of the D'Urbervilles*." v. 68, pp. 121-122; Jan., 1892.

The Spectator—"Mr. Hardy's Drama." v. 92, pp. 293-294; Feb., 1904.

The Spectator—"Literature and Journalism." v. 108, pp. 900-901; June, 1912.

The Spectator—Review of "Hardy's Works." v. 109, pp. 335-337; Sept., 1912.

Temple Bar—"In Thomas Hardy's Country." v. 108, pp. 150-153; May, 1896.

Times Literary Supplement—"Thomas Hardy's Novels." Jan. 19, 1928.

Times Literary Supplement—"Thomas Hardy, Poet." Jan. 26, 1928.

T. P's Weekly—(Listed in Saxelby's *Hardy's Dictionary*.) "Portrait Gallery XI." Dec. 31, 1909. "Thomas Hardy and His Criticism of life." June, 10, 1910. "Forces, XVIII. Thomas Hardy, Novelist and Poet." June 30, 1905. *"The Dynasts,"* Part I, Jan. 29, 1904. *"The Dynasts,"* Part II, Feb. 23, 1906. *"The Dynasts,"* Part III, March 6, 1908. Review of *Time's Laughingstocks*, Dec. 31, 1909.

Westminster Review—"Thomas Hardy's Novels." v. 119, pp. 334-364; April, 1883.

Westminster Review—Review of *"The Dynasts."* May, 1908.

World's Work—"Mr. Hardy and Our Headlines." v. 24, pp. 385-386; Aug., 1912.

The World To-Day—"Thomas Hardy." v. 51, pp. 244-245; Feb., 1928.

HARDY'S FIRST EDITIONS

DESPERATE REMEDIES, 1871. In Three Vols., Tinsley Bros., London; Vol. 1, pp. vi-304; vol. 11, pp. v-291; vol. III, pp. vi-274.

UNDER THE GREENWOOD TREE—1872; In Two Vols; Tinsley Bros. London; vol. 1, pp. 215; vol. II, pp. 216.

A PAIR OF BLUE EYES—"Tinsley's Magazine," Sept. 1872 to July, 1873. In book form 1873, by Tinsley Bros. London. In Three Vols; vol. 1, pp. 303; vol. 11, pp. 311; vol. III, pp. 262.

FAR FROM THE MADDING CROWD—"Cornhill Magazine," Jan. to Dec. 1874. In book form 1874; Smith, Elder & Co., London. In Two vols. Vol. 1, pp. iv-333; vol. II, pp. iv-334. Fully Illustrated.

THE HAND OF ETHELBERTA—"Cornhill Magazine", July, 1875 to May, 1876. In book form, 1876; Smith, Elder & Co., London; In Two vols. Vol. 1, pp. VIII-332, vol. 11, pp. VIII-318.

THE RETURN OF THE NATIVE—"Belgravia", Jan. to Dec. 1878. In book form 1878; Smith, Elder & Co., London. In Three vols. Vol. 1, pp. VI-303; vol. II, pp. VI-297; vol. III, pp. VI-320.

THE TRUMPET MAJOR—"Good Words", Jan. to Dec. 1880; In book form, 1880; Smith, Elder & Co., London; in three vols; vol. 1, pp. VI-295; vol. II, pp. VI-276; vol. II, pp. VI-259.

A LAODICEAN, "Harper's Magazine", (European Ed.); Dec., 1880 to Dec. 1881. In book form, 1881; Law, Marston, Searle & Rivingston, London; in three vols. Vol. I, pp. 312; vol. 11, pp. 275; vol. III, pp. 269.

TWO ON A TOWER—"Atlantic Monthly", Jan. to Dec., 1882. In book form, 1882; Law, Marston, Searle & Rivington, London; in three vols.; vol. 1, pp. 246; vol. II, pp. 240; vol. III, pp. 223.

THE MAYOR OF CASTERBRIDGE—"Graphic", Jan. 2 to May 15, 1886. In book form, 1886; Smith, Elder & Co., London; in two vols.; vol. 1, 313 pp.; vol. II, 312 pp.

THE WOODLANDERS—"Macmillan's Magazine", May, 1886 to April, 1887. In book form, 1887; Macmillan Co., London, N. Y.; in three vols.; vol. 1, 302 pp.; vol. 11, 328 pp.; vol. III, 316 pp.

WESSEX TALES—1888; Macmillan Co., London, N. Y.; in two vols.; vol. 1, 247 pp.; vol. 11, 212 pp.

THREE NOTABLE STORIES—1890; Spencer Blackett, London; one vol., 211 pp.

A GROUP OF NOBLE DAMES—1891; Osgood, McIlvaine Co., London; one vol., pp. vi-271.

TESS OF THE D'URBERVILLES—"Graphic", July 4 to Dec. 26, 1891. In book form, 1891; Osgood, McIlvaine Co.; London; in three vols.; vol. I, pp. VIII-264; vol. II, pp. VIII-278; vol. III, pp. vi-277.

BOOK OF THE WORDS, THE THREE WAYFARERS—(A Pastoral Play in One Act), 1893. Harper Bros., N. Y.; one vol., 32 pp.

LIFE'S LITTLE IRONIES—1893; Osgood, McIlvaine Co., London. (A few of these appeared in magazines later on.)

JUDE THE OBSCURE—"Harper's Magazine" (European Ed.), Dec., 1894, as "The Simpletons"; from Jan. to Nov., 1895, as "Hearts Insurgent". In book form, 1896; Osgood, McIlvaine Co., London; one vol., pp. VIII-520.

THE WELL BELOVED—1897; Osgood, McIlvaine Co., London; one vol., pp. XII-340; "The Illustrated London News" from Oct. 1, to Dec. 17, 1892 as "The Pursuit of the Well Beloved".

WESSEX POEMS AND OTHER POEMS—1898; Harper Bros., London, N. Y.; one vol., pp. XII-288.

POEMS OF THE PAST AND PRESENT—1901; Harper Bros., London, N. Y.; one vol., pp. XII-264.

THE DYNASTS—("*In Three Parts, Nineteen Acts and One Hundred and Thirty Scenes); 1903, 1906, 1908; Macmillan Co., London, N. Y.

TIME'S LAUGHINGSTOCKS AND OTHER VERSES, 1909; Macmillan Co., London; one vol., pp. X-212.

THE CONVERGENCE OF THE TWAIN—1912; Macmillan Co., London. (Written to aid Titantic disaster sufferers.)

A CHANGED MAN—1913; Macmillan Co., London; one vol., pp. VIII-416. (Famous for its "Romantic Adventures of a Milkmaid".)

SATIRES OF CIRCUMSTANCE, LYRICS AND REVERIES—1914; Macmillan Co., London; one vol., pp. X-232.

MOMENTS OF VISION—1917; Macmillan Co., London; one vol., pp. XII-256.

LATE LYRICS AND EARLIER, 1922; Macmillan Co., London; one vol., pp. XXIV-288.

THE FAMOUS TRAGEDY OF THE QUEEN OF CORNWALL AT TINTAGEL IN LIONESSE—1923; Macmillan Co., London. (A New Version of an Old Play.)

HUMAN SHOWS, FAR PHANTASIES, SONGS AND TRIFLES—1925; Macmillan Co., London, Greenbery, N. Y.

WINTER WORDS, IN VARIOUS MOODS AND METRES—1928; Macmillan Co., London. (Incomplete at Hardy's death and published posthumously.) One vol., pp. XI-22.

Part IV—B

HARDY'S MAGAZINE CONTRIBUTIONS

"How I Built Myself a House"—*Chamber's Magazine;* March 18, 1865.

"The Fire at Tranter Sweatley's. A Wessex Ballad."—*Gentleman's Magazine;* Nov., 1875.

"Indiscretion in the Life of an Heiress."—*New Quarterly Magazine;* April to Oct., 1878.

"The Distracted Young Preacher"—*New Quarterly Magazine;* Jan. and April, 1879.

"Fellow Townsmen"—*New Quarterly Magazine;* Jan. and April, 1880.

"The Adventures of a Milkmaid"—*The Graphic;* Summer Number, 1883.

"The Dorcetshire Laborour"—*Longman's Magazine;* V. II, 1883.

"Article on The Rev. Wm. Barners" (Obituary)—*The Atheneum;* Oct. 16, 1886.

"The Profitable Reading of Fiction"—*The Forum;* V. 5, March, 1888.

"The First Countless of Wessex"—*Harper's Magazine;* Dec., 1889.

"Why I Don't Write Plays"—*Pall Wall Gazette;* Aug. 31, 1892.

"The Science of Fiction" Part III—*The New Review;* pp. 304-309; April 1, 1931.

"Candour In English Fiction" Part III—*The New Review;* V. 2, Jan., 1890.

"Ancient Earthworks at Casterbridge"—*The English Illustrated Magazine;* 1893.

"The Spectre of the Real" (In Collaboration with Florence Henniker)—*Today,* V. II, March, 1894.

Hardy's reply to the Charge about "Georgia Scenes." *The Critic;* v. 26, n. s. p. 8, July 4, 1896.

"An Imaginative Woman"—April, 1894. Reprinted in *Wessex Tales,* 1898.

"Memories of Church Restoration"—*Cornhill Magazine;* July, 1906.

Select Poems of William Barnes, XVI-196 pp. Henry Trouwde, London, 1906

"An appreciation of Anatole France"—Dec. 10, 1913.

"The Waiting Supper"—*Murrays' Magazine.* Jan., 1888. Reprinted in *A Changed Man and Other Tales;* 1913.

"Song of the Soldiers"—Sept. 12, 1914.

"Letters on the War"—Nov. 9, 1914.

"The Dynasts"—*The Prologue and Epilogue.* Dec., 1914. Granville Barker produced an abridged version of *The Dynasts* on Nov. 25, 1914.

"In Time of the Breaking of Nations"—Feb. 1, 1915.

"The Oxen"—Published in *The Times*, Dec. 24, 1915. Reprinted in *The Homilectic Review*, Dec., 1915.

"To Shakespeare After Three Hundred Years"—1916.

"Domecilium"—Printed April 5, 1916. Earliest of Hardy's extant poems. Written about 1858.

"When I Weekly Knew;" "England to Germany;" "The Pity of It;" "I Met a Man;" "A New Year's Eve;" "In War Time."—Feb., 1917.

"The Fiddler's Story;" "A Jingle of the Times"—Oct., 1917.

"A Call to National Service;" "An Appeal to America;" "Cry of the Homeless"—May, 1917.

"Jezreel;" "The Master and the Leaves"—Sept., 1919.

Preface to "A Dull Day in London"—by Dora Sigerson Shorter, 1920.

"And There Was A Great Calm"—Nov. 11, 1918; Dec., 1920.

"Haunting Fingers;" "Voices From Things Growing;" "Two Phantoms"— Feb., 1922.

"On the Portrait of a Woman About to Be Hanged"—(Poem) Jan. 6, 1923.

"Old Mrs. Chundle"—*Ladies Home Journal*, V. 46, pp. 3-4; Feb., 1929.

"Poems"—*Literary Digest*—V. 100, p. 30; Jan., 1929.

"Division"—(Poem) *Saturday Review of Literature.* V. 6, p. 1055; May, 1930.

"Book of the Woods;" "The Three Wayfarers"—N. Y. 1893. A dramatic version of *The Three Strangers*, Terry's Theatre, London, June, 3, 1893.

"The Melancholy Hussar"—Issued first in a volume called "Three Notable Stories." Only one of these is by Hardy. Spencer Blacket, London, 1890.